The Radical Path of
Somatic Dharma

The Radical Path of Somatic Dharma

RADIANT BODY, RADIANT MIND

Will Johnson

Inner Traditions
Rochester, Vermont

Inner Traditions
One Park Street
Rochester, Vermont 05767
www.InnerTraditions.com

SUSTAINABLE FORESTRY INITIATIVE — Certified Sourcing
www.forests.org
SFI-00854

Text stock is SFI certified

Cataloging-in-Publication Data for this title is available from the Library of Congress

ISBN 979-8-88850-048-4 (print)
ISBN 979-8-88850-049-1 (ebook)

Printed and bound in the United States by Lake Book Manufacturing, LLC
The text stock is SFI certified. The Sustainable Forestry Initiative® program
promotes sustainable forest management.

10 9 8 7 6 5 4 3 2 1

Text design by Virginia Scott Bowman and layout by Priscilla Harris Baker
This book was typeset in Garamond, with Acumin, Inria Serif, and Legacy Sans
used as display typefaces

All images are in the public domain and were acquired through Wikimedia
Commons.

To send correspondence to the author of this book, mail a first-class letter to the
author c/o Inner Traditions • Bear & Company, One Park Street, Rochester, VT
05767, and we will forward the communication, or contact the author directly at
www.embodiment.net.

to everyone drawn like a moth to the flame of

the wisdom teachings of the buddhist dharma

but who find much of the current orientation

to sitting meditation a tad tight . . .

to yogis and sufis and dancers and

entheogenic explorers . . .

to the closeted mystics and spiritual misfits

among us . . .

to everyone searching for practices of

real awakening . . . .

enjoy!

i wrote this for you

ॐ~ॐ

*Someone asked the teacher Zhaozhou, "What
  is meditation?"*
Zhaozhou replied, "It's not meditation."
*The student was puzzled. "Why is it not
  meditation?"*
"It's alive! It's alive!"

JOSHU, FROM *THE RECORDED SAYINGS
OF ZEN MASTER JOSHU*,
TRANSLATED BY JAMES GREEN

Contents

■ ■ ■

"The Awakening Slave" unfinished sculpture from the series
Prisoners, or Slaves, by Michelangelo Buonarotti 1520–1523.
Michelangelo is famous for saying he worked to liberate the forms
imprisoned in the marble. On the path of somatic dharma we work
to liberate the radiance imprisoned in the still and unfelt body.

INTRODUCTION

Bound Slaves

I MAJORED IN ART HISTORY in college. It was clear that I was never going to become a political scientist, economist, or lawyer, and I exulted in the beauty and power of the objects of art I was able to feast my eyes upon and study. I even thought for a time that I might continue onto graduate school in art history and become a museum curator. At the end of my senior year I applied for admission to a graduate program and was accepted at New York University, home to one of the top art history graduate departments in North America. However, my acceptance letter was accompanied by a terse request to become fluent in German over the summer (art history as a scholarly discipline is a primarily German invention of the early part of the twentieth century, and many of its seminal texts have never been translated from German), and that request was enough to put to rest any thoughts of becoming a museum curator. I did, however, land a job in New York as an art critic for *Art News Magazine*, and for the next few years I was able, at least somewhat vocationally, to keep alive my passion for art that had been born at university.

While my college classmates were studying history and literature and language, the puzzlement of science and precise weight loads of engineering, pretty much all I was doing was falling in to a gaze with a work of art and experiencing

1

how it affected me. Some art didn't really touch me. Other pieces transported me. I was particularly drawn to the art of the Northern Renaissance, the deeply religious works of Rogier van der Weyden, and the hallucinatory dreams of Hieronymus Bosch. The atmospheric renderings of J. M. W. Turner, the lush visions of Odilon Redon, the magic of Kandinsky (in addition to his elaborate linear drawings and paintings he created abstract expressionism in the early part of the twentieth century, and no one in the 1940s, '50s, or '60s did it better), the color field artists of the mid-twentieth century—especially Mark Rothko and Morris Louis—and the explosive joy of the Pop artists all were ambrosia to my eyes. I became fascinated with how a work of art could take hold of me when I would come face-to-face with it and enter in to a kind of communion in which the rest of the world was shuttered out. Call me old fashioned but I still believe art can have an ennobling and enriching effect on human beings and that it should stun us with its beauty.

Above all these, however, a series of unfinished marbles by the Renaissance artist Michelangelo grabbed something deep in my soul and have never let me go. They were of bound slaves, heroic humans wrestling to break free from the encasing marble they were emerging out from. First of all I loved that these sculptures were unfinished as it made their rough struggle for liberation all the more immediate and visceral. And somehow even then when I hadn't yet unearthed the same struggle in myself, I felt a resonance with the heroic act of release that these figures were attempting to enact. They wanted to break free. They wanted their authentic, vibrant life back.

Over the years, as I began to awaken to how numb my personal body (and the larger cultural body as well) had become, I'd think back to Michelangelo's sculptures and view them as a perfect expression of humanity's struggle to break free from the physical, psychological, mental, and spiritual shackles that bind us and keep us imprisoned, sentenced to live out our life inside a cell of our own creation as shadows of our inherently radiant selves. All of us are kin to Michelangelo's slaves, entrapped within the bias of our somatophobic culture, struggling to free ourselves from the held and viscous tensions that have taken up residence in our bodies and choke us with their invisible grip, and the job for those of us who've become aware of the entrapment is to free ourselves from a bondage that makes no sense, to awaken our body from a dull, unfelt, stoney darkness back in to the bright light of palpable felt radiance.

The price we've had to pay for this dimming of intrinsic radiance is the nagging presence of chronic pain and a generalized sense of disease that scream out at us that we're doing something unnatural with our body. And, yet, we all figure out a way to accommodate the discomfort and make concessions for it, effectively trading radiance for something far less lustrous. Through accepting the diminution of radiance as constituting normal we've entered into a darkened cell of our own acquiescent making, and for the most part we're unaware that we're even doing this.

The bound body has three tasks in its journey from numbness to radiance. First it needs to free itself, not unlike the figure in Michelangelo's sculptures, from the marble of its cultural environment. Then it needs to go a step further and de-marbleize its entire body, awakening its altogether natural felt fluidity and shimmer, realigning itself with the flowing grain of nature, melting unbidden thought back in to silent felt presence. And finally it needs to realize that awakening the inherent radiance of the body radically transforms its sense of self and relationship to the world. You don't get the flush of radiance spreading through your body without the radical shift in consciousness that accompanies it.

The act of sitting, for minutes to hours on end, will be high-lighted in this book as the primary gesture through which we're going to explore the liberation of radiance. In most meditation practices you're instructed to sit down and then begin the meditation. In the practices of the radiant body, however, the sitting itself *is* the meditation. You don't sit down to begin a meditation technique. You sit down to explore the gesture of sitting down and, in the process, transform your sitting from a posture locked in bracing and struggle in to an altogether natural mudra of greater grace wherein awakening in to radiance has no choice but to start occurring.

The understanding and perspectives I'm going to be presenting draw largely from my exposure to the wisdom teachings of the Buddhist, Sufi, and Somatics traditions, all of which I've been fortunate to explore during the course of my life, all of which possess important keys to opening the door to our cell and showing us the way out. While the cultural shadows this liberation exposes are not happy ones I'm not interested in caviling against the inbred fear or even analyzing how we've allowed the great enslavement to occur. The goal is to break free from the entrapment, and to this end I'll present a series of meditations and practices designed to help soften and melt the fearful tensions and knots that keep us feeling so bound up.

With very few exceptions the Buddhism that is coming over to Western shores from Asia, not unlike the larger cultural environment into which it's migrating, has largely lost touch with feeling presence and is in need of revitalization, and the burgeoning field of Somatic therapy that is evolving and flourishing here in the West could well look to the wisdom teachings of the dharma for clues and guidance as to where its implications are inevitably leading. We're not here to sit like immobile statues and transcend the flesh. Nor are we here simply to feel a bit better. Putting the best of both together for those of us drawn to the task, we're here to liberate the body from bondages that deaden it and the mind from its claustrophobic compression inside an exclusively egoic perspective. To free yourself from your cultural and personal restraints and find your way back to a more felt, radiant life is the journey that I'm guessing you're already on and that I hope this book will propel you even further on.

To do this we first need to acknowledge the collective sleep that has taken us so far afield from our natural state before we can begin surrendering to the awakened currents that want to take us back home. Let's start by looking at the condition the bound slave finds itself in. It's struggling to emerge from its entrapment. It's halfway out already. But what is it about our cultural environment that so makes us want to struggle to free ourselves?

LAS DELICIAS, COSTA RICA

PART 1

The Liberation of the
Radiant Body

The Somatophobic
Entrapment

OURS IS A CULTURE that is lost in the dark passageways of thought, both bidden and unbidden, and out of touch with the felt radiant presence of the body. In order to conform to the quality of consciousness that passes as normal, and to live in the airy orbits of word and concept, we have to introduce patterns of holding and tension into the tissues of the body that in turn suppress the body's inherent felt radiance. Being lost in thought and present in awakened body are entirely at odds with each other. You can't be both at the same time. You're either one or the other, and within our culture's somatophobic bias thought always wins.

Somatophobia is exactly what it says: a phobia directed toward the soma, the felt presence of the body, the intricate shimmering web of minute sensations and felt wavelets that course through a relaxed and awakened body like water in a stream. Agoraphobics can't deal with wide-open spaces, claustrophobics just the opposite. Arachnophobics are terrified of spiders, and someone deeply enmeshed in the grip of somatophobia is both terrified of the potent felt energies of the body and irritated by how they keep on incessantly knocking and pounding on the door of awareness, begging to be let in. These altogether natural sensations and energies are potent, they're life promoting, and they want to be felt, but somatophobia doesn't want to open the door, welcome them in, and set them free.

The quality of consciousness that passes as normal in the world depends on somatophobic entrapment, and so we live shut in inside the inhibitions that the somatophobic bias implants in our body. We dial down the innate radiance of the body in order to promote a consciousness that is all too often lost in thought and wholly identified with the speaker of those thoughts.

unbidden thought is what happens
when felt sensation abdicates
radiant presence is what happens
when unbidden thought dissolves
through the reawakening of sensations
sensations and thought
are mutually repellent and incompatible
sensations melt thought
just as thought sends sensations into exile

Under the anesthetizing spell of somatophobia we all have the same name as everyone else. We call ourselves *I*, as I, after all, am the speaker of all those pesky thoughts. When felt presence is powerfully awakened the exclusively egoic perspective of the mind starts getting diluted and weakened, and the prospect of the dissolution of our egoic identity and self-image is terrifying to that identity and image. When the body awakens, when it once again makes its presence felt as a radiant glow of felt shimmer, the unrelentingly fixed singularity of the egoic perspective is revealed as not being a complete expression of "who I am." Who are you when "I" no longer dominates your consciousness? Somatophobia doesn't want you to find out.

The somatophobic entrapment that has taken up residence in all our bodies keeps us limited to but a fraction of our intrinsic radiance, and the shroud it throws over the world of awakened sensation and felt shimmer doesn't just dim our light. It hurts. Somatophobia is akin to a despotic ruler who demands that the citizens of his country adopt a set of beliefs even if those beliefs hurt them.

On every part of the body, down to its smallest cell, minute, subtly tingling, buzzing, carbonating, fluidly vibratory sensations can be felt to flicker on and off, but only if they're allowed to make their presence felt, and the somatophobic bias of our culture doesn't really want you to become aware of them, let alone support you in doing so.

Which begs the question: why? What could possibly be so offensive about the awakening of these altogether natural, often highly pleasurable, and powerfully healing energies and sensations? The simple answer is that their explosive awakening reveals a secret door beyond which the bias of somatophobia doesn't hold sway. What's on the other side of the door? Like being in a video game and moving to a new level, a path gets revealed that, if followed, can lead to a radical awakening of who and what you experience yourself to be and how you understand your relationship to the world you live in, and this new awareness will lead to an unraveling of somatophobia's tight grip. It will eventually lead to a reckoning of everything that you are (sensations don't lie): the good, the bad, the ugly, the beatific. As sensations start making their formerly hidden presence felt, the physical compression and tensions that support the somatophobic entrapment can expose themselves, and once felt, they can start coming undone.

To awaken radiance you're asked to empty your pockets and leave at the door your beliefs about yourself, the yarns that the egoic perspective so compellingly, and effectively, spins about you. You're asked to start *feeling* what you are directly and forgo the thoughts about what you *think* you are. You're asked to relax your exclusive attachment to the egoic perspective—your sense of "I," the most embedded thought of them all—and realize that it's not the only setting on the camera lens of consciousness and doesn't represent everything that you are.

So conditioned are we to worship our "I" and so completely are we identified with it that the prospect of its suspension and its replacement by something else—even if that something else is deeply healing of the body and salving to the soul—causes us to roll our eyes in disbelief as to why anyone would want that for themselves. This is how ingrained the amnesia of our somatophobic entrapment has become.

Children mimic their parents who mimicked their parents, and so the entrapped holding patterns of somatophobia get passed down seamlessly from one generation to the next. At every turn the somatophobic model gets reinforced right from the very moment of our entry into the world up to the moment of our passing beyond. We can't escape it. We're all somatophobics.

We worship superficial beauty (we idolize the personas of our stars and starlets, the impossibly fascinating-looking models who catwalk along the runway) yet remain compliant to an unspoken message to dim the body's inner radiance. Our obsession with beauty at the surface of the physical body is inversely reflected in our antipathy toward the deeper energies that want to awaken and eventually burst forth in radiance, and this fear and irritation are strong enough, and so culturally dominant, that these energies are mostly kept contained, held in, unfelt, and unexpressed.

Somatophobia imprints its stamp on all of us. It shapes our body, our breath, and consciousness itself. Despite our individual differences and unique life stories, our personal aspirations and fears, it affects all of us in an alarmingly similar way and makes us very much alike. It's as though a somatophobic cookie cutter has molded the doughy shape of all our bodies. Then we add the chocolate bits, the nuts, the raisins, the smarties that make each one of us unique as well. No two snowflakes may ever be identical, but on the surface they all look pretty much alike.

The way we stop ourselves from feeling anything is to freeze and hold the body still. Unsurprisingly somatophobia's preferred strategy for blocking the inherent radiance of sensation is to implant a holding pattern of frozen stillness throughout the tissues of the body. The stiller you become, the less you feel sensations. The more effective you become at embodying a somatophobic holding pattern, the more you withdraw in to the corners of your mind where unbidden thought and egoic identity rule the roost. So pervasive is the imposition of patterns of tension and the frozen stillness that perpetuates those patterns, and so accepted as normal, that for the most part we're not aware of it even though these ingrained patterns of constant tension cause pain.

Please don't misunderstand. There's nothing inherently wrong with the egoic perspective. This is the consciousness that allows you to function in the world of form where all objects are eternally separate (and *I* is a stern marker of separation), and it's important that you get good at it. The only problem with the egoic perspective is that it believes it's the only perspective that could possibly exist and is highly effective at making you believe that as well, and this is where ego's deceptive fib entraps you and exposes itself as hopelessly narcissistic. Ego is in love with itself and wants you to honor that love with equally unwavering devotion, never allowing your affections to stray to the alternative perspectives of consciousness that naturally emerge out of a radiant awakening of the body.

The consciousness of the egoic perspective gets locked into place through a constant tensing of the orbicularis oculi, the muscles surrounding the eyes. Unrelaxed we look out onto a world through a crimped lens, so that what we see is a distortion of what might otherwise be there to be seen. Chronically unrelaxed ocular muscles help create the image we have of ourselves and ensure that we stay attached to it. This self-image is like a smoky picture show that appears on a phantom screen projected out at the front of your face that only you can see. Self-image—your mind's eye picture of who you are—appears on this filmy and invisible screen that divides the you inside here from the world outside there, the place from which you see from that place out onto which you look. It filters. It interprets. It projects. It rarely just observes. Chronically tense orbicularis muscles support the primacy and exclusivity of the self-image. The tension locks you there, in this bifurcation that creates an "I and the rest of the world," and so we identify as "real" an exclusive diorama of separation.

Being lost in thought depends for its existence upon the chronic tensing and contraction of the temporalis muscles, the seashell-shaped muscles on either side of the head just above and behind and a bit lower than the auricular opening where the vibration of sound meets the sensitive hearing mechanisms in the ears.

Anyone who has ever entered into an anechoic chamber realizes there's no such thing as true silence. Anechoic chambers are the quietest places on Earth, but they're hardly silent as you become overwhelmed by the vibratory hum of the body, the whooshing sounds of internal liquids, the incessant beating of the heart. We live in a sea of sound the way fish live in a sea of water. Sounds loud and small, sounds distant and near, sounds coming from somewhere inside you. Yet, lost in thought, you block out sound, from both exterior and interior sources.

So accustomed are we to being lost in thought and identified with thought's speaker that we mostly aren't even aware of how unpleasant this chronic contraction feels. Even so, somato-phobia doesn't want you to relax the tensions in the cranium because relaxation of the contraction puts somatophobia's "candidate of choice" for the consciousness that it wants to promote as "normal" at risk of unraveling and melting down. Nor does somatophobia want you to value the real sounds of the world in which you live over the silently heard monologue of random and unbidden thought that makes its pronouncements inside your head, as turning your attention to sound immediately relaxes the temporalis muscles. As the contraction through the orbicularis and temporalis muscles relaxes, so also does the egoic perspective's exclusivity and the silent storylines that sustain it.

The highly limiting effects of somatophobia can also be felt in how the breath, the very source of life, gets restrained and held back under stultifying patterns of tension that get implanted into the tissues of the body. We take in enough oxygen to keep our bodies alive but not to support and unleash their radiance. Under the rule of somatophobia the diaphragm, the complex horizontal muscle that separates the upper and lower torso and is the source origin of breathing, gets dramatically cramped and constrained, its motions minimized. It stays far stiller than it needs and is designed to be, and hence respiration stays much smaller than it could be.

Our bodies are possessed by an impulse to move, and yet the somatophobic bias of our culture inhibits that impulse. Sit still. Don't be too expressive, and certainly don't venture in to spontaneous expressions of radiance. Under the spell of somatophobia the body freezes, limiting its natural sense of organic motion, as though it's been poured into a mold with no amoebic tendrils of motility.

Chronic patterns of tension and holding create a vibratory frequency, not unlike a radio setting, that once tuned and locked into keeps on transmitting programs of being lost in thought and out of touch with felt presence, and we keep on listening to its droning broadcasts 24/7. Another way of saying this is that we have to introduce patterns of painful tension in to our body in order to tune in to the consciousness of lost in thought.

The contemporary version of the bound slave on the path of liberating itself first needs to reconnoiter, acknowledge its situation and environment—the sticky, treacly, viscous medium of held-back energies and numbed sensation—and assess how it's going to get free. So when you sit down you start by just feeling what's there to be felt. It's okay to feel the tension, the holding, the numbness, the stillness, the discomfort, to be aware of how the parade of random thought keeps jerking you around, to actually feel what somatophobia has done to your body, breath, and consciousness. It's hardly a spoiler alert to tell you that it doesn't feel good, and so it's understandable why most of us don't want anything to do with examining its consequences. But somatophobia feeds on itself. The more you keep resisting something, the more you fuel its power over you, the more twigs get added to the somatophobic beaver dam inside you. You have to bring its effects to felt awareness before you can begin its dismantling. Otherwise you stay removed from what needs to let go.

Don't Try

sitting still
frozen
as little motion as possible
don't try to change a thing
can you become aware
of how small your breath is
how still your body is
how your thoughts are running
how little you feel your body

The Line

SEQUOIA TREES KNOW ABOUT THIS. Oak trees don't seem to care. The architects of the Gothic cathedrals knew about this. The builders of the earlier Romanesque churches were still searching for it. Children with wooden building blocks know about this. As grown-ups we mostly forget.

Out of a near infinite number of linear possibilities there exists only one directional coordinate, a kind of sweet spot, capable of transforming the gravitational pull of the Earth from a force against which you have to brace into a force that supports the letting go that blossoms in to radiance. That coordinate is the axis of verticality, and it is so important for the liberation of radiance in the human body that we can capitalize it and call it The Line.

I remember back to a time when I was a young child and liked to play with brooms. I was fortunate to have been born into a family that had a summer cottage on a lake, and my daily chore was to keep the outdoor patio of our cottage swept and clean, free of the falling leaves and branches that would drop down onto its surface. I enjoyed the chill tranquility of the freshly cleaned patio, its surface completely clear of random litter and droppings. I liked feeling the accomplishment of a task completed. And I especially enjoyed, as a kind of reward I suppose, playing with the broom, balancing it upside down on my upturned, outstretched palm at the conclusion of my chore. Balancing an upside-down broom on my outstretched hand was my first direct experience of The

Line as I would move my hand here and there, in tinier and tinier increments until—ahhhhh!—the magical moment in which the broom just stayed suspended in the air. It just floated there, apparently defying Earth's possession of it. As soon as the long shaft of the broom's handle started to deviate even in the slightest from The Line, the broom would begin to wobble this way and that, and I'd have to get busy again, moving my hand slightly here, slightly there, trying to stop its fall, coaxing it back to its floating upright position in space or watch it crash to the floor.

The Line is as sacred to the builders of skyscrapers as pi is to mathematicians. Of all possible numerals, of all possible directional coordinates, they possess an aura of the mystical. Without pi mathematicians would be at a loss to relate to a circle. Without an understanding of The Line architects and engineers couldn't build a multistoried building. And without exploring how an investigation into The Line can affect your body, reshaping how it wants to position itself in space, you'll remain handicapped in your attempt to liberate radiance. As The Line has no palpable existence other than as an invisible structural coordinate, it's like an imaginary friend who is nonetheless very real for the seeker of liberated radiance, a constant companion even if no one else can understand or even see your close encompassing friendship with it.

Objects whose upright structure is organized around The Line no longer have to brace themselves against gravity. This is as true for human bodies as it is for giant sequoia or redwood trees, but in humans an exploration of The Line provides an additional bonus. Optimizing your relationship to gravity through figuring out how to organize the structure of your upright body around an imaginary vertical axis also directly catalyzes the awakening of the body's felt presence.

You can't think your way in to this harmonization of your

physical body with The Line. You can only dance and feel your way in. You can't stand in front of a mirror and try to shape your body, from the outside in, in to what you think The Line is. The Line is an inside job. You explore it through responding to the sensations that emerge as you play with the subtle dance of upright balancing.

> *how tall can you be*
> *how relaxed can you be*
> *how effortless can you be*
> *in being as tall and relaxed as you can be*

Exploring The Line you no longer have to brace yourself and resist the pull of gravity. You can let go instead, throughout your entire body, and still stay sitting or standing upright. In every successive moment of playing with The Line sensations and felt awarenesses emerge and morph. Like metal detectors that sweep a popular beach in search of hidden jewels and coin and go off when their operators come across something of value, The Line lets you know through the medium of sensation if you start hovering around it or, equally, when you're nowhere near its grace.

It's not possible to overestimate or over-acknowledge the importance of this understanding if you truly wish to awaken your birthright of radiance and free yourself from the tensions and holdings that keep your body bound and your mind limited. The Line tells you that it's okay to let go and allows you to do just that. You don't need unnecessary tension anymore. You can sit or stand upright not through bracing, but through playing with upright balancing, just like the sequoia tree, just like my childhood broom.

Why is an embodied exploration of The Line of such critical importance to the liberation of radiance? The simple answer is that it allows you to relax and let go in a way that isn't possible if the upright shape of your body deviates from the vertical in any major way. What you're able to relax and let go are not just the physical tensions that you conventionally rely on to keep you sitting or standing upright but the mental and emotional tensions that have also taken up residence in the tissues of the body. These tensions, no matter their source, keep radiant shimmer dulled and enshrouded. What you relax out of is a straightjacket that's kept your feeling presence dialed down and your mind cloudy and limited. What you relax in to is a world alive with vibratory sensation and the felt awakening of powerful energies deep inside you.

Think back for a moment to my childhood broom. Once the long shaft of the broom found The Line and locked itself into the sweet spot of the vertical, it would appear to defy the law of gravity that draws all objects to itself and instead float effortlessly in the air above my outstretched hand. That moment of suspension felt timeless. But as soon as the verticality of the shaft was lost the broom would start angling all over the place—right, left, forward, backward, circling, jerking—and I'd frantically have to compensate for its lean as I attempted to bring it back to the upright vertical or, more often than not, watch it topple to the floor, hoping that it wouldn't take a lamp or vase with it.

The practices of the radiant body always begin with a felt exploration of The Line. No more chronic bracing as you sit or stand, no more struggling, just honing in on that sweet place as though your upright body was the shaft of the broom. Relaxing and letting go, no longer having to brace yourself against yourself and the pull of gravity, is the gestural key that unlocks the prison cell of your bound self, and The Line presents you with that key. It's like a Get Out of Jail Free card. You don't have to struggle heroically to liberate radiance. You don't have to force anything to release. You just have to play with balance and let go. Just as you can't use the mind to dissolve its hold on you, neither can you use tensional force to resolve tension. Playing with The Line, you can drop your weight, let go, and feel how the Earth not only supports you, but lifts you up.

There are two Laws of Gravity, but mostly we're only aware of the first. The gravitational pull of the Earth draws all objects to itself, and we're all privy to this first law. We don't go floating off into space, and when the coconut falls from the tree, it falls straight down, hopefully not bonking any unsuspecting animal resting underneath it. Everyone knows about the first Law of Gravity.

The second Law of Gravity is known by very few people. It tells us that even though all objects are drawn to the Earth, the effect of gravity can be altered through a felt exploration of The Line from being a force against which you have to physically brace yourself in to one that allows you to relax your bracing and experience yourself as buoyed up instead.

Subject only to the first law, we struggle against gravity. Awakening to a direct experience of the second law, we discover how it can also lift us up. As the Kularnava Tantra says: *as one falls to the ground, one must lift oneself by aid of the ground.*

As a body hovers around The Line and lets go, softening its tensions because it no longer needs to resist the gravitational tug of the Earth, a shaft of palpably radiant energy gets stirred and starts flowing through its length. An embodied exploration of The Line is the *mahamudra*, the *great gesture* of the body. It liberates a flow of energies that, however momentarily, washes away the exclusivity of the egoic mind and the fixity of the somatophobic entrapment dependent as they are on tensions not only in the cranium but throughout the entire body.

❧❧

Koans are alogical puzzles, statements, questions, or riddles that students of Rinzai Zen spend long hours and days mulling over until a breakthrough occurs. The koans of radiant body practice can be thought of as somatic koans, suggestive puzzles that you explore through your body and lead to felt awakenings.

The Koan of The Line

the practice of the radiant body
always begins
by exploring the koan of The Line
and experiencing how it affects you
stand up
imagine there's a vertical shaft of light
that passes through your upright body
starting in the ground underneath you
passing all the way up and out the top of
*   your head*
connecting heaven and earth
feel your body
make spontaneous motions
to organize its upright structure
as effortlessly and efficiently as possible
around this vertical shaft of light
wobble slightly at your ankles
to the sides
forward and back
just as though you were a broom shaft
finding its way to the upright
tensions block the transmission
of this upright shaft of light
so keep letting go
to let the light pass through

ॐ

sit or stand as tall as you can
while remaining as relaxed as you can

you can't just preen
or reach for height
with muscular effort
like a child backing up to a doorjamb
being measured on their birthday
to see how much they've grown in a year
or a ballet dancer on a stage
seeking length and grace
you can't just collapse either
releasing all the bracing
you normally need
to stay upright
as without the vertical alignment
of your body when you stand
of your torso when you sit
you would just fall over
engaging The Line
introduces you to a subtle dance
of spontaneous adjustments
the dance of balancing
embodying simultaneously
two apparently contradictory qualities
tall and relaxed
lifted up
surrendered down
breath by breath
sensation by sensation
you just keep playing

dancing with The Line
The Line is there inside all of us
just waiting to be discovered and explored

tension enshrouds sensation
keeping you lost in thought
and out of touch with felt presence
as The Line lets you release no longer
    necessary tension
sensations come out of hiding
back into felt life
pass your awareness through your body
part by part
take a moment
and feel into every little part
just feel
just sensation
no need of a mental picture
of that part of your body
just sensations as they are
by simply turning your attention
to a part of the body
like shining a flashlight
into a dark corner
sensations begin to reveal themselves
and arise in that part of the body
tingling
buzzing
shimmering
oscillating
pulsing
vibrating

rippling
rushing
painful
pleasurable
strong
delicate
alive
take your time
and invite sensations to appear:
the top of your head
your entire scalp
your ears
your forehead
your eyes
your nose
your mouth
your cheeks
your chin
just invite sensations
exactly as they are
to make their presence felt . . .
your neck and throat
your shoulders
your upper and lower arms
your hands
your fingers
the front back and sides of your upper torso
the front back and sides of your lower torso
just invite the sensations that are there
to make their presence felt . . .
your entire pelvis
your openings of elimination and procreation

your upper legs
your lower legs
your feet
your toes
the whole body altogether
as you play with The Line
extend a loving invitation
to each and every part of your body
to come back to felt life
sensations waking up
subtly tingling
throbbing
shimmering
body awakening
welcome unexpected ecstasies
the pleasure of shimmer
welcome unexpected discomforts
the compression of shimmer

and then
immediately greet the acceptance of your
     invitation
from any part of the body
with a gesture of relaxation
just let go
soften
melt
relax
feel tension melting and expanding
outward into space
throughout the entire body
invitation to awaken

gesture of relaxation to let go
let the continual relaxing of emerging
  sensations
be your primary guide
in figuring out a response
to the koan of The Line
tall
relaxed
as effortless as possible
all at the same time
keep finding the next least effortful place
breath by breath
dancing around the upright
become a truly upright human
upright in physical stature
upright in the fundamental decency
of your awakened felt nature

Sitting and standing are both perfect bodily positions for exploring The Line and experiencing the awakening in to radiance that its embodiment stimulates. When we stand we dance. When we sit we meditate, but when we sit with The Line, we sit more like a subtly sinuous dancer than a stone garden statue of the Buddha. Radiant body meditation practice is as akin to what happens when you explore a yoga posture as it is to more traditional meditation practices. It's an ongoing inquiry in to *padmasana*, the sitting posture of hatha yoga, bringing the body ever more vibrantly alive as, breath by breath, sensation by awakening sensation, everything keeps morphing, unfolding, evolving.

Your mind can't tell you how to do this. Only awakened sensations can guide and show you the way. You have to shift the pull of your attention from thought to sensation. You can't pry your way in to The Line from the outside in. You can only relax your way in to it from the inside out.

Imagine for a moment that you live in a sea of gravity (you do). Can you be like a seahorse, floating upright as it makes its way through its watery medium? This isn't just a romantic image. Syncing in to The Line generates a felt sense of buoyancy or lift even while remaining tethered to the ground underneath. Pondering the koan of The Line lets you confront the somatophobic entrapment head-on where its bias is exposed as profoundly limiting.

In the Satipatthana Sutta, one of the earliest texts of Buddhism whose words are often attributed to the historical Buddha himself, the very first instruction on meditation that he gives is to sit with the spine erect and upright. The Buddha knew about The Line! He understood its importance in supporting the transformation. It is both paradoxical and tragic that the most common posture in the southeast Asian schools of Buddhism where that Sutta is still revered is all too often a posture of collapse instead.

The eleventh-century Indian-born, Tibetan mahamudra teacher Tilopa also clearly knew about The Line through his encouragement to *become like a hollow bamboo* whose unobstructed interior creates an unblocked central passageway for the awakened energies of the body to pass through, much like water through a garden hose. When these evolutionary energies can be felt to flow through the long interior shaft of the body, they naturally radiate outward. What was formerly pale becomes radiant.

As schoolchildren it was always so annoying to hear teachers berate us to "sit up straight." But there was never the follow-up payoff to not only sit up straight but to activate the felt gesture of relaxation throughout the entire upright body. No wonder we all rebelled as young students, and yet this is where the early admonitions to sit or stand up straight have left us.

There's nothing magical about The Line, even if it at first looks to be so to the young child in awe of the upside-down broom balancing on top of an outstretched hand. It's simple structural engineering applied to human evolution, healing, and the liberation of radiance. Exploring how the upright structure of your body spontaneously organizes itself around the imaginary vertical axis of The Line, you can let go of unnecessary tension and yield to the current of liberated radiance that wants to sweep through your body like a flash flood.

Can you remember back to a time in your childhood when you carried a friend on your shoulders? When you put them down, you felt a pronounced lightening throughout your upper body almost as though you were floating upward. Whenever you drop a burden this sensation of lightening is your reward.

Because you no longer need to brace yourself against gravity to stay upright The Line lets you drop your weight and surrender it to gravity's omnipresent tug instead. Tensions that are no longer necessary start dropping away. Body comes alive in awakening shimmer. And suddenly you start feeling literally uplifted, from the inside out, almost as though you were being drawn upward by a force analogous to the Earth's gravity but acting in the opposite direction from it. You enter in to the lightening, just as you did when you set down your friend that you'd been carrying on your shoulders.

Enlightenment (en-lightenment) is literally an entrance in to the lightening. Drop your unnecessary burdens and enter in to the lightening instead.

Undulation

THE IMAGE OF AN UPSIDE-DOWN BROOM suspended in the air paints a graphic picture of how important The Line is, but to more fully experience how a felt exploration of The Line can affect and transform your body, you need now to move beyond the rigidity of the broom's wooden shaft. In a human body The Line is not like a fence post. It's more like what happens when you ride a bicycle. It's a verb, not a noun. Or, in the manner of a saying from Yoda, the Star Wars sage: *there is no balance; there's only balancing.*

You're not just wanting to become as tall and straight as you can be and stay frozen there like a soldier standing at attention. You're also wanting to evoke relaxation (just as the eleventh-century Tibetan teacher Tilopa encouraged in his Song of Mahamudra that contains in one pithy sentence the whole of the teaching: *do nothing with the body but relax*), and to truly relax, everything in the body needs to keep subtly moving and undulating. The liberation of radiance depends on a gesture of relaxation extended through time, and relaxation is not a static condition. It's an ongoing, ecstatic (ex-static) one. You don't just relax or let go as a one-off gesture. Relaxation and letting go are stream events. You enter the stream of relaxation and get carried along on its currents like a leaf in a flowing brook. Much like balancing itself relaxation is a verb, not a noun.

If the body remains completely still there can be no real

relaxation and, hence, limited radiance. The body under the spell of the somatophobic entrapment becomes stiff and frozen, bringing tension in to its tissues, stopping breath in its tracks, and feeding the already out of control parade of random and unbidden thoughts in the mind. The radiant body is a pulsing, thrumming, amoeba-like body, continuously in motion, constantly expanding and contracting on the breath, never coming to standstill. If ever that constant motion stops, tension replaces relaxation, and the radiance of the body's shimmer suffers.

Tall and relaxed is constantly shifting and morphing. It's an ongoing dance, not any kind of fixed condition or permanent state. Just as it cannot be overemphasized how important The Line is in the liberation of the radiant body, neither can it be overemphasized that The Line in a human body is constantly changing its shape, continuously undulating, more like a fly rod in motion than a Maypole covered over with pretty streamers.

The spine is composed of twenty-four individual bones called vertebrae, and the joints between them are no different from joints anywhere in the body. They're there to allow the adjacent bones to move.

The spine isn't like a column from a Greek or Roman temple. As strikingly beautiful as the remains of those temples may appear, they're inanimate objects, and the chief feature of inanimation is that nothing moves. The spine is a column in the temple of the body, and the radiant body's form of prayer at this columnar temple is the allowance of undulation.

The eighteenth-century Swedish mystic Emanuel Swedenborg, one of the very first Westerners of record to grasp the power of the breath, was looked upon by the citizens of Uppsala as a kind of living saint. Swedenborg attributed much of his personal awakening to his belief that the purpose of the breath was to keep the spine in constant motion. Swedenborg was a contemporary of Lavoisier in France and Priestley in England—the fathers of modern chemistry, who came to understand how the oxygen in the air we breathe is primary fuel for the body—but was unaware of their discoveries. Much like the historical Buddha, some twenty-three hundred years earlier, Swedenborg viewed the breath as a medium for awakening. In the undulating body breath keeps softening the tension and frozen holding that keep the spine more like a Greek or Roman column than a human one.

Breathing the Spine

come to standing
place your feet fairly close together
pay particular attention
to the sensations of contact
between the soles of your feet
and the ground on which you stand
this place of literal understanding
feel the long shaft of your body
rocking gently back and forth
at the ankles
over the feet
keep allowing spontaneous adjustments
to your exploration of The Line
pass your awareness
through your body
from your feet
to your head
feeling the awakened sensations
of the segments of the body
stacking themselves
one on top of the other

feet
legs
pelvis
torso
neck
head
feel the long shaft of the upright body
as a unified field of felt presence
feel how you can hover
in this awakened upright
just like my childhood broom

now transform the broom
from a static shaft
into an alive
motile
moving
flexible
willow pole
movement all along its length
as you breathe in and out
invite motion to occur
at each and every joint
between the vertebrae of the spine
as you inhale
the lumbar spine
composed of the vertebrae in your lower back
can relax and lengthen
the thoracic spine in your upper torso
can relax and lengthen
the cervical spine in your neck
can relax and lengthen

on the exhalation
the entire spine can shorten back down
lengthening on the inhalation
shortening on the exhalation
tall and relaxed fluctuating
along the axis of the vertical
in resilient response
to the cycle of breath

where in your spine
can you allow and feel motion
as you breathe in and out
where in your spine
do you feel more frozen
without any motion

now sit down in a posture of meditation
explore The Line
invite sensation to awaken
relax the newly felt sensation
and start feeling how the entire body
can rise and fall
on the breath
lengthening up through the spine on the
    inhalation
settling back down on the exhalation
up and down
constantly moving
lengthening
shortening
never coming to a sitstill
the whole body

as a radiating field
of felt presence
riding up and down
on the cycles of the breath

notice that the moment this altogether natural
     motion stops
tension gets reintroduced
the spine becomes more frozen
you leave the shimmer of felt presence behind
and go off in random and unbidden thought
center yourself
in the felt presence of your moving spine
rather than the thoughts in your cranium
still spine
moving thoughts
moving spine
no thought

When you first begin the practice of Breathing The Line, you're as likely to notice areas of your spine that don't seem to move very much at all as you are to come across areas that move freely. Don't fret or become discouraged that your spine doesn't move as freely as Swedenborg envisioned. We all begin our loosing of radiance in a body that's been molded and formed within the somatophobic bias of our culture. To express the quality of consciousness that passes as normal within a culture entrapped in somatophobia, you have to hold the spine relatively frozen and still. The first awakening in to how still you actually hold your spine can be humbling and exciting both. Don't feel bad because you discover areas of lockdown. Awareness of where, in your compliance to the somatophobic bias, you do freeze adjacent vertebrae is enormously valuable on your journey toward radiance. Frozen tension is an impeccable guide pointing you to the precise location that needs to be relaxed and released. First you have to feel the places in your body where you're frozen before they can begin to melt.

This promotion of a moving spine in sitting meditation practice is completely different from the approach to breath awareness in most contemporary Buddhist schools. In many of the current teachings—whether from the Vipassana, Zen, or Vajrayana traditions—you're instructed to sit down as relatively still as possible, like a stone garden statue of the Buddha, and observe your breath as it enters and exits the body. Yes, most teachers will tell you to relax, but it's not possible to truly relax without inviting undulation in to your sitting posture.

In the Satipatthana Sutta the Buddha instructed us to begin our journey of awakening the breath by simply observing it as it enters and leaves the body. And he also instructed us to carry out this observation *at the front of the body*. While a good deal of the current teaching about breath in the Buddhist world both begins and ends with this observational practice, the Buddha's instructions don't end there. They culminate a few short sentences later in the altogether remarkable suggestion *to breathe through the whole body*, not just to concentrate on how it can be felt to pass in and out of the nostrils or cause the front of the belly wall to rise and fall slightly.

As your awareness of breath's never ceasing passage in and out becomes more refined, your focus naturally starts broadening all by itself. No longer so narrowly concentrated on one little part of the front of the body, you now start becoming aware of how breath can be felt to interact with progressively more and more of the body until its effects can ultimately be felt . . . everywhere.

When there's no awareness of breath mind loses itself in thought and self-image. When you become more vigilantly aware of breath at the front of the body mind starts awakening to itself. When the whole of the body becomes involved in the action of breath you start glowing in radiance.

To breathe through the whole body you first have to feel it, to awaken the shimmering web of minute pin-prick blips and wave-lets of sensation that can be felt to buzz and hum and tingle and flow through every cell of your body. And so you play with the dance of upright balancing and pass your awareness through every part of the body, inviting sensations to come out of hiding, greeting every sensation that's accepted your invitation with an immediate gesture of relaxation.

> *like stars coming out at night*
> *sensations blossom*

Second you want to allow responsive motion to occur at the joints of the body so the force of breath can be transmitted through the body's entire length. Allowing undulating motion to occur throughout the spine spreads relaxation throughout the body as everything immediately adjacent to the spine can begin to move in response. The ribs move. The shoulders float. The head bobs up and down. The pelvis rocks.

Undulating Breath

sit down in upright meditation posture
on a chair
on a kneeling bench
or cross-legged on supportive cushions on the
*   floor*

make sure that your sitting bones
are elevated higher than your knees
in this way you create a stable base of support
for the upper torso
to float effortlessly upright
on top of the pelvis
take some time
as you bring the body
to wakening
feeling how The Line
lets you become ever more effortless
how sensations come back to felt life
and are immediately greeted
with the gift of relaxation
remember
the spine is a moving column
as it lengthens and shortens
rises and falls
in response to the cycles of the breath
it undulates
uncoiling on the inhalation
recoiling on the exhalation

at the onset of inhalation
relax your body so deeply
that you feel your lower torso expanding
rocking forward
in front of your sitting bones
as your lumbar spine lengthens
at the onset of exhalation
rock back
behind your sitting bones

rocking forward
rocking back
in coordination
with the cycle of breath

turn your attention
to your shoulders and head
at the opposite end of the spinal column
at the onset of inhalation
surrender the weight of your shoulders and
    head
to gravity's gentle tug
just let go
your shoulders drop and may move slightly
    forward
while your head dips momentarily toward your
    chest
and then is drawn effortlessly backward
and gets lifted
your shoulders float
making spontaneous motions
as the head bobs through the cycle of breath
if you can let go in this way
a much larger volume of air
comes rushing into your body
as air rushes in
it creates buoyancy and lift
your head circles backward and rises slightly
as your cervical spine lengthens
at the onset of exhalation
shoulders retrace their motion
the head relaxes and starts coming back down

its momentum picking up as the next inhalation
  rushes in
the key to releasing the head
from its statuesque hold
is to relax and release the shoulders
if you keep your shoulders rigid and still
like a wooden yoke sitting atop an Asian water
  buffalo
the head can't move
and you remain stuck in your thoughts

the lower torso
rocks forward and backward
over the pelvis
never coming to stillness
the head
viewed from the side
traces a small bobbing circle
never coming to stillness
the shoulders float to their own rhythm
now start allowing
all three movements
to occur simultaneously
rocking forward and behind the pelvis
bobbing the head in a small circle
in conjunction with the meandering motion in the
  shoulders
as a surrendered response
to the cycle of breath
when all of these
completely natural and relaxed motions
can occur simultaneously

you will feel
the entire spine naturally undulating
between the poles of sacrum and head

the key
to the initiation
of undulating breath
is to express a gesture
of complete letting go
throughout the entire body
at the very onset of inhalation
you just let go
you surrender
the entire weight of the body
to gravity's gentle pull
you just let go
into the felt presence
of the whole of the body
you just let go
you literally drop your mind
as the physical tension that sustains it in your
cranium
is given permission to just let go
as you do this
a far greater volume of air
naturally enters your body
enlarging your body
lengthening
lifting you up
while securing you into the earth
and the simultaneous rocking over the pelvis
the bobbing of the head

and the free motion in the shoulders
are experienced not so much
as actions you perform
but as actions you allow

the secret
to unleashing the potency
of undulating breath
is to coordinate the full range of motion
with the fullness of breath
if you stop moving
before you stop breathing in or out
undulation stops
and you get locked back in
to the parade of unbidden thought
if undulation and breath
begin and end together
a plug gets pulled
on the parade of thought
and the sense of self
that identifies
as the speaker of the thoughts
just keep exploring the natural motions
that occur in a relaxed body
over time they can become
second nature to you

if you think
that perhaps you're not really allowing
much undulating motion to occur
freeze everything
don't let anything move

the lower back and pelvis frozen
the head
ribs
shoulders
still
feel how much more constricted
held
limited
this contrasting posture is
the spine frozen
the breath impeded
so just let go again
and start allowing
these completely natural undulating motions
subtle and small as they may be
to occur in response
to the inhalation and exhalation of breath
the not uncommon pains
in the lower back shoulders and neck
of sitting meditators
are largely a function
of holding the pelvis shoulders or head
rigidly still
and not allowing the spine to undulate
the practice of Undulating Breath
is of central importance
to the liberation of radiance
as it provides the skill set
for learning how to let go

The following ode to the fullness of breath was found as an inscription on stone from the Zhou dynasty, 500 BCE:

in transporting the breath the inhalation must be full
when it is full it has big capacity
when it has big capacity it can be extended
when it is extended it can penetrate downward
when it penetrates downward it will become calmly
*   settled*
when it is calmly settled it will be strong and firm
when it is strong and firm it will germinate
when it germinates it will grow
when it grows it will rise upward
when it rises upward it will reach the top of the head
the secret power of providence moves above
the secret power of the earth moves below
whoever follows this will live
whoever acts against this will die

The beauty of undulating breath, whether you're sitting in meditation or walking in town, is that the inhalation presses down through the legs in to the Earth while simultaneously lifting the torso and head up toward heaven. On the exhalation the motion retracts.

up and down
up and down
up and down
the whole body constantly moving

Clark Kent's grey flannel suit keeps his deep nature wrapped up and contained. As he bursts out of his conventional clothes his radiant power explodes open and lets him leap tall buildings in a single bound.

Such is the nature of myth. Let's bring that back down to you and me. The awakening of radiance, unlike in Superman, has nothing to do with the release of superhuman powers. You don't fly like a bird or soar in to space like an airplane. You can only use the emergence of radiance for its ability to heal the pains of your body, both physical and emotional, and to open your eyes to the alternative dimensions of consciousness that's available to human beings. The introduction and allowance of spontaneous, natural, amoeba-like motion in to the posture of meditation is the proverbial idea whose time has come to the Buddhist world where so much instruction is directed toward sitting still with as little movement as possible.

When you're lost in thought, your body becomes as still as the 1904 sculpture of Rodin's "The Thinker." When you relax and let go, when you surrender to the whole of body's felt presence, everything begins subtly to move and consciousness begins to shift, to open, to expand, to awaken. The moving body is like the expanding universe. When sensations are awakened, the ensuing gesture of relaxation can be felt to keep expanding indefinitely outward. That expansive glow only gets dimmed when the conventional mind of thought and identity, and the tension and stillness that support them, reassert themselves.

Chronic pain resists the breath and the current of the life force, both of which want to pass freely through the conduit of the body like a wave passing through a body of water. Where this passage gets blocked—through tension and frozen holding around the joints of the body—pressure builds. The current of the life force gets jammed and presses against the restrictive tissues. You don't have to "break through" these stuck places. You only need to let their feeling presence emerge, yield to the intensity of sensation that's contained within them, and surrender to the subtle motion that's been held back for so long. Chronic

First bronze casting of "The Thinker (Le Pensuer)" by Auguste Rodin in the garden at the the Musée Rodin in Paris, 1904. The consciousness of being lost in thought depends on the frozen stillness of body, nothing moving.

pain doesn't move. It's like a black hole that sucks motion and life force out of surrounding tissue. So you want to allow the natural motions that you've inadvertently been holding back on to come back to life and start occurring not only through the spine but throughout the entire body.

Radiant Body, Radiant Breath

BREATH AND BODY are direct reflections of each other, different mirroring expressions of the same phenomenon. A body that's frozen and stiff blankets over the felt shimmer and breathes very shallowly. A body that allows amoeba-like motions to occur throughout its length resurrects the shimmer and allows a much fuller, and far less restricted, breath to come alive.

> how your breath is
> your body will be
> restricted breath
> frozen body of tension
> liberated breath
> radiant body of undulating motion

Liberating the radiant body is also, then, a function of liberating the breath from its imprisonment in tense, inert, frozen, and unmoving flesh. It's not possible to liberate the full, felt majesty of the body's intrinsic radiance without simultaneously liberating the breath. And so the Buddha's culminating instruction on breathing tells us to *breathe through the whole body*, every little bit of it, experiencing how breath can be felt to touch in to, interact with, and pass through the entire body, head to foot, leaving no little part out.

The following two practices directly support the awakening of a breath that breathes through the whole body. The first practice, Virtual Acupuncture: The Portal Meditation, can powerfully stimulate the awakening of sensations throughout the entire body. The second, Breathing in the Six Directions, promotes constant motion. Done together, they powerfully catalyze the awakening of radiance.

Virtual Acupuncture: The Portal Meditation

sit down in upright meditation posture
evoke The Line
tall
relaxed
effortless
everything starting to move
enter into the dance
of upright balancing
now imagine
that you're inserting two acupuncture needles
one on either side of the spine
at the level of the lower back
as your needles press lightly inward
you start to feel
a spreading glow of awakened sensation
expanding around the imaginary points of
     insertion
let the needles
be your very pointed invitation
for sensations to awaken
don't concern yourself
as to where the precise point

where you insert your needle
should be
there's no such thing
with this practice of virtual acupuncture
as the precise point or place
wherever you feel
to insert your imaginary needle
is the perfect place for you
so just insert your needles
and feel the blossoming of sensation that occurs
insert two more needles
on either side of the spine
at the level of the middle back
insert two more needles
toward the outside of either shoulder blade
insert two more needles
on the inside of either wrist
make sure you place your imaginary needles
into the felt flesh of your body
rather than in your mind's image
of that part of your body
in this first section of virtual acupuncture
the placement of the needles
can be seen to create a constellated image
like stars in the night sky
of a weeping willow tree
a central trunk rising up either side of the back
spreading outward and down to the wrists
feel the constellated points
and the space between them
all at once

࿎

place an imaginary needle
in the back of your neck
remembering that wherever you place your needle
   is the perfect place
place an imaginary needle at the very top of your
   head
place another imaginary needle in your forehead
in the region of the third eye
feel how the placement of this needle
draws your relaxation inward
stimulating the pineal gland
place two more imaginary needles
in the right and left temples
just lateral to the eyes
in this second section of virtual acupuncture
the placement of the needles
can be seen to create a constellated image
of multiple intersecting triangles
keep cycling your feeling awareness
through each of these points individually
then go back to cycling through
each individual point
melting the tensions
in your cranium
so responsible for staying
lost in thought
and identified with self-image
how many triangles can you trace
and feel into
the more you're able to feel relaxed glow
in all these points simultaneously
the more conventional mind of thought dissolves

ﻬ

place an imaginary needle in the soft notch
just above the sternum
place an imaginary needle
somewhere in the middle of the belly
between the belly button
and the bottom of the sternum
place two more imaginary needles
at the front of either side of the pelvis
around the bony protuberances
of the anterior superior spines of the pelvis
in this third section of virtual acupuncture
the placement of the needles
can be seen to form an image
like an upside-down dowsing rod
or perhaps the eiffel tower
feel the constellated points
and the space between them
all at once
and keep releasing tension
and liberating energies
where the needles bring your attention to
throat
heart
belly
pelvis

place two imaginary needles
on the outside of the ankles
just a bit behind and beneath the ankle bones
lightly place an imaginary needle
in the perineum

inhaling strongly into this sensitive point
in this fourth section of virtual acupuncture
the placement of the needles
can be seen to create
an image of a triangle lying on the ground
if you're sitting cross-legged on cushions
or an image of a leaning upright triangle
if you're sitting on a chair or kneeling bench
creating stability at your base
over which the other constellations can hover

go back and tweak each of your imaginary
   needles
lower back
middle back
shoulder blades
wrists
back of the neck
top of the head
forehead
sides of the head
sternal notch
upper belly
either side of the front of the pelvis
outside of the ankle bones
perineum
as you tweak each needle
feel the body both awaken and relax
through each of these points

now feel all the needles at once
the whole body stimulated

become aware of sensation awakening
not only in the points of insertion
but in the space between the adjacent points
       as well
as you breathe in
breathe into all of the points
at the same time
as you breathe out
release tension from all of the points
at the same time
every one of these points
can be experienced
as a portal or gate
out of which
sensation can pour and blossom
and into which
you can feel magnetically drawn
into a sense of vast internal space
keep exploring the geometries
of both tangible body
and internal space
when you can feel the activation
of all the points
all at once
you create a constellation
throughout the entire body
of a Tibetan stupa
trust your body to make the decisions
as to where needles should be placed
delete or add needles
as you like

ॐ∽ऽ

Breathing in the Six Directions

sit down in upright meditation posture
start playing with The Line
imagine that your body is a balloon
you can fill with your breath
the physical stuff of the body
is the shell of the balloon
the breath breathes into
the interior space of the balloon
begin by filling up
the lowest section of your balloon
through a strong inhalation
that causes the lower back
to expand backward and elongate
take a number of breaths
expanding and lengthening the lower back on
  the inhalation
just as though you're blowing up a balloon
retracting the lower back on the exhalation
just as though you're emptying a balloon
take several breaths
feeling the front of your belly
expanding forward on the inhalation
retracting on the exhalation
just as though you're blowing up and emptying
  a balloon
take several breaths
feeling the right side of your belly
expanding outward on the inhalation
retracting on the exhalation
just as though you're blowing up and emptying
  a balloon

you may have to rotate your torso to the right slightly
as you breathe in in this way
rotating back to center as you exhale
take several breaths
feeling the left side of your belly
expanding outward on the inhalation
retracting on the exhalation
just as though you're blowing up and emptying
    a balloon
you may have to rotate your torso to the left
as you breathe in in this way
rotating back to center as you exhale
now take several strong breaths
feeling the four directions
of this lower segment of the balloon of your body
from your perineum below into the diaphragm
    above
expanding on the inhalation
retracting on the exhalation
just as though you're blowing up and emptying
    a balloon

move your awareness to your chest
take several breaths
feeling the back of your upper torso
lengthening and expanding backward on a strong
    inhalation
shortening and retracting on the exhalation
now take several breaths
feeling the front of your chest
expanding forward on the inhalation
retracting on the exhalation

now take several breaths
feeling the right side of your chest
expanding outward on the inhalation
retracting back in on the exhalation
again you may have to rotate your torso to
    the right
as you breathe in in this way
rotating back to center as you exhale
now take several breaths
feeling the left side of your chest
expanding outward on the inhalation
retracting back in on the exhalation
rotate your torso to the left
as you breathe in in this way
rotating back to center as you exhale
now take several strong breaths
feeling your entire chest
from the diaphragm below
right up into the neck above
expanding outward on the inhalation
retracting on the exhalation
just as though you're blowing up and emptying
    a balloon

the diaphragm
is the top of the first section
the bottom of the second
all too often the diaphragm is frozen
with very little motion
inhibiting the full range of breath available
    to you
let your diaphragm

expand and contract in all four directions
like the wings of a manta ray
as it swims through a body of water
when the diaphragm breathes
like the wings of a swimming manta ray
the lower torso section of the balloon
and the upper torso section of the balloon
have no choice but to expand and retreat
    effortlessly

move your awareness up into your neck and head
take several breaths
feeling the back of your neck and head
relaxing
as it can be felt to lengthen and expand
    backwards
on a strong inhalation
retracting on the exhalation
now take several breaths
feeling the front of your throat and face
relaxing
expanding
billowing forward on the inhalation
right out through your face
retracting on the exhalation
now take several breaths
feeling the sensations in the right side of your
    neck and head
expanding outward on the inhalation
retracting on the exhalation
rotate your head slightly to the right
to allow the expansion on the inhalation

returning to center as you exhale
now take several breaths
feeling the sensations in the left side of your
    neck and head
expanding outward on the inhalation
retracting on the exhalation
rotate your head slightly to the left
to allow the fullest expansion on the inhalation
returning to center as you exhale
now take several strong breaths
feeling your entire neck and head
expanding outward in all four directions on
    the inhalation
retracting on the exhalation
just as though you're blowing up and emptying
    a balloon
to fill the balloon of your cranium
you need to relax whatever tensions
are there to be felt
in the back of your head
in the front of your face
on either side of your cranium

now expand all three segments
lower torso
upper torso
neck and head
in all four directions on the inhalation
contracting on the exhalation
just as though you're filling and emptying a
    balloon
feel everything at once

filling
emptying
expanding
contracting

now add the last two directions
up and down
on the inhalation feel the energies of the
     body
simultaneously pressing down into the earth
while rising up through the top of your head
connecting earth and heaven
on the exhalation
the body can be felt
to once again shorten
as the energies from above and below
are drawn back into the diaphragm
and finally let your inhalation
expand your entire body
in all six directions
just as though you were blowing up an entire
     balloon
let everything contract back down
on your exhalation
just as though you were letting the air out
of an entire balloon
the whole body breathing
the whole body moving
subtle
continuous
amoeba-like motion
that never comes to a standstill or sitstill

❧

as you continue to breathe in the six directions
once again go through your body
and tweak your imaginary acupuncture needles
breathing strongly
into and out of the points of insertion
the whole body shimmering
the whole body moving
experience the bliss
of the radiant body

Random and unbidden thought can only appear in a body that resists this natural motion at one or more of these places in the body. So long as everything stays naturally moving in resilient response to the breath, you can't get lost in thought. Another way of saying this is that the consciousness of lost in thought can't hit a moving target. As you explore Breathing in the Six Directions, you'll find that it's easier to experience expansive and contractive motion in some places more than in others. After a while let yourself steadily, but not aggressively, lean in to the stuck places with your inhalations. Just touch in to those places through your breath. Whenever breath touches in to a part of the body that's stuck or tense, healing occurs.

Breath as Bodyworker

use your breath
like the internal equivalent
of a bodyworker's hands
a bodyworker touches you
from the outside in
breath touches you from the inside out
on the inhalation

lean in
into the areas in your spine
that don't move much
the places in your tissues
that restrict the breath
never try
forcibly to create motion or sensation
in any area of your body
just inhale into that area
as fully as possible
relax
and be on the lookout
for motions that want to occur
never try
to force a tension to let go
just breathe into it
let the breath create motion
where formerly there was none

Just as the spine is not a column from an ancient temple, neither is the ribcage a medieval suit of armor. Composed of twenty-four individual bones (twelve on each side) that wrap around the body with attachments at the vertebrae in back and, with the exception of the lowest ribs, the sternum in front, the ribcage is designed to move, expanding outward as you inhale and drawing itself back in as you let the breath out. The only way this altogether natural movement doesn't occur is if you tense and freeze the musculature of the rib cage, turning its tissues in to the hardened strips that a mummy gets wrapped in rather than letting the bands move freely on the breath. Exploring the following practice as a somatic koan supports you to let go completely of any holding in the body and mind that restricts the breath.

a body
is something wrapped around a breath
let the wraps flow freely
like silk scarves

IDA ROLF

If you think of the fleshy mass of the body as something wrapped around the breath, you can feel the encasing mass relaxing and releasing outward on the inhalation, wrapping itself back in on the exhalation.

Unwrapping the Breath

start by unwrapping the ribcage
breath by breath
the ribcage expanding and contracting
then unwrap the entire body
unwrap the tension that inhibits The Line
unwrap the tension in your cranium
that keeps you lost in thought

Breath never unwraps itself and reveals what's hidden underneath in a straight line. It constantly gets shorter, longer, pulses, builds and subsides. As you continue to let go, the posture of sitting meditation, once thought of as becoming still as a rock, turns in to a continuous dance of subtly undulating motion. Body naturally torques and unwinds as tensions unravel. The head may rotate to one side or the other and back. The torso may twist slightly to one side on the inhalation and back to center on the exhalation. The body may bob back and forth, side to side, on your sitting bones. Freed from its fixations, moving breath becomes a cleansing cloth, touching in to hidden holding everywhere in the body and relaxing the wraps of holding's frozen grip from the inside out.

The teachings of traditional dharma are as pertinent today as they have been for twenty-five hundred years, but somewhere along the way the teachings about how to sit in meditation have become rigid, promoting a frozen stillness that fosters tension, not relaxation. When spontaneous motion replaces stillness, when sensation and breath waken from their collective slumber, when The Line is invoked, meditation comes alive.

Surrendering to Current

I'M GUESSING THAT many of you who are reading this book have had the good fortune, much like me, of attending Vipassana retreats, Zen sesshins, or Vajrayana dhatuns. I will be forever grateful that the teachings about transformation born from an unbroken 2,500-year inquiry in to the very same issues of self and consciousness that so fascinate you and me have come in to my life.

I'm also guessing that, again like me, many of you may have felt perplexed over the years as the revelations that the Buddha said were all of our natural birthrights weren't coming as quickly and clearly as you'd hoped and the amount of severe discomfort and pain you may have felt sitting for long hours and days at retreats, sesshins, and dhatuns just seemed unnatural. When sitting practices first came in to my life, there were times I felt despondent over the frozen walls that I couldn't seem to deconstruct or pass through to get to where I knew the revelatory awakenings reside. And the amount of physical pain that I would routinely feel during long retreats left me really pondering if this was a path I wanted to pursue or not.

The way sitting is mostly taught and promoted in contemporary schools of meditation can unwittingly subvert the altogether natural transformation that the practices are designed to evoke. Little real instruction on posture is ever offered in most schools other than a cursory "sit down in a position that is comfortable to you." I certainly could have benefitted from far more specific guidance on how exactly to do that and ended up over the years having to figure out some basic principles of sitting posture on my own. Without knowing about, exploring, and incorporating these simple somatic principles, many of us suffer unnecessarily during long retreat.

The Taoist poet Chuang Tzu once declared "easy is right," and one of my primary inquiries over the past fifty years has been in figuring out how to make the practice of sitting ever more user-friendly. The unexpected and significant bonus to this inquiry has been the realization that the principles that were shown to me along the way don't just make our time on the cushion, kneeling bench, or chair far more comfortable. They also take us far more deeply and rapidly in to the revelation realms of the teachings. Taking the orientation of the radiant body in to Vipassana retreat, Zen sesshin, or Vajrayana dhatun makes it far easier to experience what those teachings are telling us.

Even though most contemporary approaches to sitting do not explore the fundamental principles I've presented in this book, the ideas themselves aren't anything new. Nor are they in any way a radical departure from instructions on meditation that can be found in the traditional texts. They're already all there, writ large, in the traditional teachings. It's just that, somewhere along the way, we've forgotten them or haven't quite put the pieces together:

> *sit with your spine erect and upright*
> *do nothing with the body but relax*
> *and breathe through your whole body**

---

*The first and third lines are from the Satipatthana Sutta, one of Buddhism's earliest texts whose words are often attributed to the historical Buddha himself, and the middle line is from Tilopa's Song of Mahamudra, one of the seminal texts of the Tibetan mahamudra tradition.

I couldn't possibly say it any better or any more succinctly. This is the practice. Through these principles we let go of the rigidities and impositions of the stone-statue-of-the-Buddha approach to meditation and become far more gracefully alive in our sitting.

In the beginning of practice it's helpful to parse out and focus on the individual pieces and components that together form the foundations of radiant body meditation: The Line, the awakening and relaxation of sensations, undulation. As you become ever more familiar with how each one affects you, they naturally start catalyzing one another, and you eventually find that you're no longer exploring each on their own, separate from one another, but playing with all of them at the same time:

> *you can't really explore the upright*
> *without awakening the body*
> *and allowing motion to occur*
> *you can't really relax the body*
> *without playing with an upright that moves*
> *you can't really allow transmitted motion to occur*
> *without relaxing into the upright*
> *sit in meditation*
> *and play with all three facets*
> *of the one jewel*
> *breath by breath*
> *at the same time*

The shimmer of the awakened body flows like water through a tube. Individual sensations join together into waves that can be felt to pass through the watery medium of the relaxed body, building here, receding there, ebbing, flowing, morphing, sloshing around, like the shifting currents in a river. As the foundational practices come together, sensations can be felt not just flickering on and off but flowing in waves through the body, and it's now up to you to just . . . let go and ride the moving currents. No one can teach you how to do this. You have to figure it out for yourself. The best anyone can do is offer strategies and suggestions as to how to get you to the river so you're able to jump in. Did you ever jump into a stream as a child and let the current take you? It's exactly the same with radiant body practices except that the currents are inside you.

Think of the foundational practices that have been presented up to this point in this book like scales that jazz musicians need to become proficient at so when they go out on stage, they can truly let go and play.

The great twentieth-century body-oriented meditation teacher U Ba Khin suggested that awakening the shimmer (what he referred to as activating *annica*, the felt experience of constant, vibratory change) would in its turn expose and liberate a force whose evolutionary purpose is to shepherd us to the furthest shores of realization available to humans. He called this force *nibbana dhatu*, the force of enlightenment. Unlock and untether this force, he would suggest, and then ride upon it as it melts blockage to the free flow of sensations passing through the body.

I like to think of nibbana dhatu as the current of the evolutionary life force that over long millennia, if Darwin is correct, has kept propelling us to an ever more upright posture accompanied by ever greater mental capacity. When this force gets powerfully activated you start feeling a strong and palpable current streaming through you. Body becomes a river of rushing sensation, pouring itself out in to the world.

As U Ba Khin suggests this current is here to heal and enlighten you, but you have to unlock the blockages to its flow and quit resisting it, letting it move through you instead, however it wants and at whatever pace it adopts. Once you feel the current starting to flow, your job on the cushion is just to let go and ride the current like a surfer rides a wave.

This palpable evolutionary force exists in each and every one of us but lies mostly dormant and restrained. We can try to keep it at bay (and somatophobia is very good at this), as though we're more immovable an object than it is irresistible a force, but let's be honest: resisting something far more powerful than we are is never going to work well.

> *forces never stand still*
> *they can be directly felt*
> *they're powerful*
> *and they always move*

In the center of your body an explosive force of felt sensational awakening is hibernating, waiting for you to thaw your resistance to it. As soon as that resistance begins to melt and that force begins to awaken, your body will start to move. Sometimes the movements are subtle and small, a Buddha body simply expanding and contracting on the breath. Other times they may be more akin to what we normally associate with spontaneous movement or dance. Sometimes they start to reach and stretch. Sometimes archetypal parts of yourself—the sad child, the chip-on-a-shoulder youth, the wise elder, the criticizer—emerge to play themselves out in a kind of psychodrama. How do you deal with these impulses both subtle and large? You let go to them and let them move you. I have no idea why bodies move the way they do when they're exploring these practices. It's not necessary to know. Just surrender to the force and let it move you.

ॐॐ

The awakened currents are eventually going to take you everywhere in your body, in to every little nook and cranny, in to
places where joyous shimmer and freed motion suddenly pop up
like rainbows after a rain shower as well as in to historical and
cloudy residues of compacted tension that keep shimmer and
breath contained.

> ride the alternating waves
> let the current keep moving through you
> unraveling the knotted ball of yarn
> that is the somatophobic body
> carrying you along with whatever it unearths
> free flowing streams
> rapids that scare you silly
> just keep going

As the wraps release and the knots come untied, everything
that they were keeping contained and held in can start coming up to the surface of felt awareness where they can be freed
and released. The first delicious awakening of the shimmer is
only the opening act as sensations beget more sensations that
keep leading you down into ever deeper layers of somatic mate-
rial. Programmed somehow into the data cloud of the body's
tissues is a record of all the emotional content and memories
that we never felt safe or honest enough to feel and express
in the moment. Whenever it feels unsafe to allow the expression of natural emotion, we squelch its emergence through
bringing tension in to the body, creating in effect a protective
firewall that keeps the unacceptable emotion contained and
unexpressed.

But what happens to the energy of the emotion? Just because
we don't allow its expression doesn't mean that it goes poof and

disappears. Nothing ever goes poof and disappears (which is why J. Robert Oppenheimer, the father of the atomic bomb, came to believe in reincarnation for, as he said, energy can't just up and disappear). The energies are sent instead down in to soma's dark storehouse where they tend to fester inside a protective layer of enmeshed stillness. Locked away and repressed we may not be able to feel their presence or even remember them but we're always at their effect.

The path of the radiant body doesn't just liberate sensations like soft falling rain. It frees up everything that you've been holding back on: ecstasies and terrors alike. Unwrapping the breath inevitably reveals whatever you've wrapped up and sent away. Know that whatever comes out of hiding as you continue to let go in your practices is ok. Just keep letting go through your breath.

As you continue in your practice, you will always keep coming back to the foundational principles, but then when the shimmer is reawakened and the current unlocked, you can just go along for the ride, simply letting go at the onset of inhalation, allowing whatever breath and motions need to come through you at that moment.

Inevitably there will be many, many moments when you wake up belatedly to the realization that you've gone off in thought once again, patterns of held and frozen tension have snuck back into your body, and you're holding back on the breath. Don't be so quick to try to resurrect radiant awareness. Exploring lost in thought lets you discover what you unconsciously do in your body to plug back in to the quality of consciousness that passes as normal in the world: compacted in self-image and thought in the cranium, out of touch with body. Ah, hold that moment that you've just woken up to, and *feel* what resistance to the current of the relaxed life force actually feels like. Really feel it. Watch how body tenses and breath is held. This is your most familiar holding pattern. It's where you live much of your life.

And then, without forcibly changing a thing, slowly go back through your fundamental koans, like a pilot going through their check list before taking off. Slowly. See how the foundational principles affect you. It may take many breaths as you gradually resurrect a felt awareness of The Line, the deeply awakened and relaxed, the motility, and experience thought evaporating. The goal of the practice is not to be free of fluctuations. The goal is to keep riding the changing currents.

So where does stillness have a place in the practices? In honoring the traditional teachings it has to be said that the familiar practices of narrowing your attention down onto a tiny little part of your body—the most common example being the nostrils where breath can be felt to enter and leave your body—are most easily entered into in a body that is holding itself relatively still. Stillness muffles the shimmer that, strongly awakened, would be intrusive on a mind that solely wants to focus its entire attention on one small part of the body. The stillness of a body that can focus its attention in this way also, of course, curbs the breath. In the Theravadin practices of *anapanna* that focus on the nostrils, breath generally slows down and gets smaller and finer, and there are definite benefits to this. Mind becomes more concentrated back inside your head where you're safer from the cascades of random thought that want to lure you out of yourself. It's easier to stay mindfully aware when you're not moving around too much.

The subsequent instructions, though, steer you away from narrowing your focus and keeping the breath slight. Quite the opposite, in fact. They tell you to relax and broaden the focus of where you experience your breath to now include the entire body. As your surrender to the breath naturally evolves, you free up motions that focusing so narrowly has caused you to stifle.

Stillness also plays a role in the practices of the radiant body which aren't just about opening to the spiritual revelation we will address in Part 2 of this book. They're also about personal healing, and the two are inseparably connected. Chronic pain is resistance to the radiant current of the life force that wants to stream through the conduit of your physical body like water through an open sluice. Opening the floodgates on the evolutionary current exposes everything deep inside that you haven't wanted to feel and have been holding back. Layer after unexpected layer of historical trauma that stillness attempts to conceal can suddenly start flashing back up in to felt life, revealing itself, and you either run from it and attempt to stuff it back down into its muffled box or greet its emergence with as much acceptance as you've learned to greet emerging shimmer.

The eruptive felt surfacing of a powerful layer of long-held tensions, resistances, stored emotional content, and energetic blockage always occurs in conjunction with a sudden freezing of body and breath somewhere along breath's cycle (visualize a mime's expression of fear: a sudden, startled, sharp inhalation that then freezes while the eyes bulge). When a layer of primal contraction bursts in to felt life, it literally takes your breath away. You're suddenly frozen in the intensity. You can't move or breathe.

So what do you do now? It would seem that the practice of the radiant body is always about liberating and welcoming ever more motion: subtle, natural, organic motion. While this understanding is one of your primary guides as you explore the practice, it's also important to remember that the practice is ultimately about letting go and riding the ever-changing currents of sensations moving through the body. It's not about blasting through anything, forcibly trying to change anything, striving for anything, or creating some kind of higher condition of body and mind. It's really just about trusting that whatever you've let go in to is exactly what you need to be experiencing. Giving yourself permission to actually feel how deep your patterns of holding are is what jumpstarts the process that transforms held tension back in to shimmer and motion.

If moments of seizure pop up out of nowhere, accept and receive them. Don't resist them, and don't fight with them. Enter into their intensity. This is where the awakening of body has taken you. Never force the breath to come back to "breathing through the whole body." The intensified sensation is itself the doorway to its own resolution. Stay . . . stuck. And wait. Feel in to the compressed intensity and emotionality. Let it be. No breath. Just wait. Don't run from the intensity (we've been doing that our entire life). Wait. Wait. And eventually the next phase of the breath comes, and without forcing anything or trying to change what's happening you can slowly invite more undulating motion back in to the frozen state.

Frozen eruptions are not your enemy, a sign that you've lost your way. They're the path. Sometimes the intensified emergences self-liberate easily through the breath. Other times it takes much longer, but know that the place inside yourself that you probably least want to have anything to do with is actually the doorway to where you most want to go. Behind that door powerful energies of healing are just waiting to be liberated and explode open.

Heaven and hell both live inside the body, but mostly we reside in a kind of pale limbo that avoids either extreme. Not wanting to go anywhere near the intense contraction that lies hidden at the core of our body, we block the flashing opening in to felt radiance that is all of our birthrights.

As you keep playing with the dance of upright balancing and keep relaxing emerging tensions, a moment may come when the whole body explodes open in radiant presence and conventional mind simply melts away. These moments of what might be called *somatic satori* (in traditional Zen, satori is a moment of sudden, radical awakening) are as powerful as anything you've ever felt, so delicious as to be almost unbearable, as intensely blissful as emerging contraction is painful.

Enjoy those moments, but don't lust after them or do yourself the disservice of thinking that the goal of the practice is to live there forever. As wonderful as these moments can be, they're not the goal that you're seeking. The goal is to ride upon the tidal currents of the river of your life force as it builds, subsides, ebbs, flows, dips, and soars, now dropping down in to hell, now rising up in to heaven, now stabilizing yourself on the Earth. Experiences both pleasurable and painful come and go. The current of the life force flows on forever.

∂•⌀

> *ol' man river*
> *dat ol' man river*
> *he must know sumpin'*
> *but don't say nuthin'*
> *he jes' keeps rollin'*
> *he keeps on rollin' along*

The wonderful Oscar Hammerstein chorus from the 1927 Broadway musical *Show Boat* could easily be a meme instruction for the practices of the radiant body. Through an embodied exploration of the foundational principles, you become aware of the felt current of the life force that wants to move through you. Sometimes like an amoeba that subtly expands and contracts on the cycle of the breath. Sometimes more dancerly as the body gets in touch with a gesture of letting go that allows unpremeditated, spontaneous motion to occur as in Indonesian *latihan* or the liberated motions of Emilie Conrad's *Continuum*. Awakened body is not a thing. It's a river.

As long as you can keep the locks to the canal of the river open, the egoic perspective no longer has solid ground on which to stake its claim to being the only condition of consciousness that anyone in their right mind would ever want anything to do with. It starts loosening its grip, giving up its occupation of your head, and what replaces thought is a flowing river of sensations that can be felt passing through the cranium.

In this way the practices encourage you to be, as the Buddha suggested, *a lamp onto yourself.* No one told the first human how to stand up on their two legs. When the time was right, they just did it. Yielding ever more to the current is to become a light onto yourself as you're the only person who can show you how to choose letting go over bracing.

I like to think of the Sufi word *fana* not as an annihilation, as it is most often translated, but as *the river where the I disappears.* On the Theravadin path in southeast Asia, practitioners who start awakening are referred to as *stream-enterers.* No longer an exclusive entity, a particular *I*, the stream-enterer palpably experiences that life is more like a flowing river passing through the body. Nothing fixed. Just flow.

The Line leads you eventually to the river. It all starts there, with an inquiry in to how verticality and a gesture of upright balancing opens doors that you may have never even known existed. In acknowledgement of the blessings that The Line bestows on those of us who welcome its influence into our lives, lets bookend this small section with another old song lyric, another meme instruction for the practices of the radiant body, this one written by Nat King Cole and Irving Mills in 1943:

straighten up
and fly right

Paying initial attention to the play of upright balancing when you first sit down on your meditation cushion, kneeling bench, or chair is the first item on your "pilot's check list"—the effortless upright (check), the evocation of relaxed felt shimmer (check), the notion of motion (check)—that ensures that your practice is about to take off safely and successfully on your evolutionary journey in to The Great Wide Open.

PART 2
·········
The Great Wide Open

The Consciousness of
Felt Radiance

IN THE FIRST PART OF THIS BOOK we've addressed how the quality of consciousness that passes as normal in the world, so often lost in random thought and firmly identified with the silent speaker of all those thoughts, depends for its existence on a pattern of tension and bracing that forms barriers against the free flow of the body's awakened waves of sensation. The Sufi mystic Rumi labeled this condition of mind and body *the consciousness of separation*. It could also be called *the consciousness of the egoic perspective* as *I* is a consummate demarcation of separation: me inside here, everything else outside there. While it's important that we get good at this dimension of consciousness in order to function effectively within the world of form in which no two objects can ever occupy the same space, our acquiescence and addiction to it comes with a price. Believing it's the only dimension of consciousness worth inhabiting, and persuasive enough to keep us believing this as well, it keeps us confined within itself, compressed within the thought space of the cranium where we're out of touch with the life-affirming sensations of the body.

Rumi also tells us that we can free ourselves from the entrapment, that we can melt away the tensional barricades that leave us feeling pained, numbed, oblivious, confused, alienated, or claustrophobically compressed and that create such an uncoupled separation between *you* and everything perceived to exit outside your physical body. Not surprisingly, as the entrenched bubble of separation with which somatophobia encases us starts going pop through the relaxation of the tensions that create and support it, the consciousness of separation also loses its autocratic grip and starts getting nudged aside by what Rumi calls *the consciousness of union*. I like to call this condition The Great Wide Open as the shuttering doors that keep us contained get opened as wide as the sky. A body that's liberating its physical radiance and breath suddenly finds itself floating inside this altogether natural, but radically different, dimension of embodied consciousness. Even if just for a little minute the bound slave is free.

While the consciousness of a body out of touch with its felt radiance mostly remains identified with the speaker of all the thoughts that pass through the mind, a body that has awakened radiant presence begins to express, altogether naturally, an alternative condition of consciousness that has been referred to as *tathata* in Mahayana Buddhism, the *nondual state* in Advaita Vedanta, *rigpa* in Dzogchen, fana—the river where the I disappears—in Sufism. William James, the American religious philosopher, spoke of it as *sciousness*, a condition of pure awareness devoid of the need for the intermediation of the concept *I*. All of these, as well as The Great Wide Open and Rumi's *consciousness of union*, are fundamentally identical, different ways of acknowledging the same reality. They all point to the existence of a dimension of consciousness entirely natural for a human being to experience but mostly blocked by the prejudices of the somatophobic bias. If somatophobia ruled the lepidopteran world, it wouldn't want to support the caterpillar to break free of its encasing shell. The cocoon would get somehow hardened and resist the birthing of the butterfly.

The consciousness you're expressing in this moment is a direct reflection of what you're doing with your body. The expression of emotion erupts spontaneously, without any need for language. Anger, sadness, or joy are all dependent for their expression on differing bodily gestures, and the same holds true for The Great Wide Open. In a holy moment of felt awakening in which currents of shimmer can be felt to awaken and flow freely through the entire body, a plug gets pulled on the parade of unbidden and random thoughts that so easily commandeer consciousness. When thoughts go, so also goes the speaker of those thoughts, and radiant consciousness exposes a dimension of being in which, even if only momentarily, I—my conventional sense of who I am, my identity as (insert your name here), with all my attributes, my talents, my good features, my not so good features, my personal history—just vanishes. No more self-images. No more speaker of the no more thoughts. No more filters. No more judgments or interpretations. No more projections. As *I* gives up its dominion and your body erupts in felt flows of sensation, the familiar contents of mind dissolve, and you become more of a clear and impartial mirror that registers whatever's placed before it: the visual field, the sounds, the sensations. Just this . . . with nothing added or taken away, alive in immediate sensory awareness and a pervasive sense of enjoyment.

As body continues to awaken, the domination of *I* continues to weaken. Since *I* creates an immensely powerful intermediary veil separating *me inside here* from *everything I look out onto out there*, the whole perceived edifice of separation starts unraveling along with it. The consciousness of union—which you're genetically wired to experience yet culturally discouraged from going anywhere near—suddenly appears not as some kind of abstract platitude (*we are all one*) but as palpable felt experience. Visual field, awakened sensation, and sound all collapse down in to one another, a crack in the fabric of the world of appearances is exposed, and you slip right on through in to The Great Wide Open.

Creative thinking is one of the great achievements of our species, but the apparently unstoppable parade of random and unbidden thought that seems to go on forever is one of our greatest banes. I had the good fortune to know the philosophical psychologist Julian Jaynes as a mentor and friend in university. His groundbreaking book *The Origin of Consciousness in the Breakdown of the Bicameral Mind* gives as fascinating an account of the origin of thinking as anything I've ever come across. On one classically idyllic afternoon, sitting on the grass with our backs resting up against a tree, he turned to me and asked: "Do you ever wonder where your thoughts come from or even why you think at all?"

I remember feeling stunned by the question. My honest and embarrassed response was uh-uh, not really, in fact not at all, never even considered anything like that, but the posing of that loaded question did have the effect of launching me on an inquiry in to the mechanics of thought that has continued all my life.

Jaynes hypothesized that thousands of years ago, as language and communication became increasingly more sophisticated, humans started becoming aware of voices inside their head. The words that were being created through vocalization started being silently heard inside the cranium. The appearance of these voices only happened to a few select people who were looked upon as the new priests of the emerging culture, emissaries through whom, it was believed, the gods were directly speaking. Slowly this new faculty became far more commonplace until it exploded over time in to a universal function shared by everyone. And so here we are today with our inability to stop the thinking mind from issuing its increasingly banal and annoying commentaries.

If in a time long ago the appearance of voices was an unusual occurrence, a direct message from the gods, the torrent of thoughts that have taken up residence in all of our heads is anything but. If you're really paying attention closely, it goes on and on almost nonstop. And so we block our awareness of it so as not to hear the offending din, like a radio that's been left on for so long that we manage not to hear it.

So conditioned are we to somatophobia's effects on the body that we're mostly unaware of the tension, especially in the cranium, that's necessary for thought to form. Ordinarily we think of the body as the animal below the neck and the head as something different, the human repository where thought takes place and soul, if there is such a thing, is situated. But there's absolutely as much sensation and shimmer in the cells of the cranium as there is in the body below. Tension is not something you feel just in the muscles of your neck and shoulders, your upper torso and belly, your pelvis, your arms and legs. Tension exists every bit as much in the tissues in your cranium as anywhere else in the body, and that tension needs to be indefinitely prolonged for you to function solely within the consciousness of thinking, whether you're creatively and consciously musing or simply going along on autopilot on random and unbidden thought streams. So necessary is it to the creation of the consciousness that passes as normal in the world that you no longer feel how still and achy, how impairing to the free flow of the radiant life force it is.

Once it's freed up through the awakening of the shimmer, the current of the life force wants to pass through the entire length of the body like water passing unobstructedly through a hose. Not unlike a drilled well of water or oil when the liquid is first discovered and freed, the awakened current of sensations in a deeply relaxed body can even be felt to billow and flow right up in to your cranium and out through your face and head. For this to occur, you have to soften and melt the tensions and resistances in the cranium that function like a cork in a bottle.

The physical foundation of The Great Wide Open is a body that has awakened, even if only temporarily, a unified flow of shimmer that can be felt passing right through its entire mass from the bottoms of the feet up through the top of the head. No more division between body below the neck and head and thoughts above.

thought does
to the free flow of sensation
what a lock in a canal does
to the free flow of water

replace thought with felt flow
through relaxing the tensions in the cranium
that are necessary for thought to exist at all

Uncorking the Wine

begin this practice
sitting or standing
playing with The Line . . .
exhale completely
blow all the used air out
all of it
blow out even more
than you think you can . . .
wait . . .
now let go

inhale deeply into your belly and pelvis
right through your legs
and down into the earth
breathe down into and through
the lower part of your body
feel the sparkle of felt shimmer
extend down into the earth
tethering you there
as you surrender and let go
to the incoming inhalation
feel the lumbar spine expand and lengthen
and do nothing with the upper body but relax
as breath grounds itself into the earth
it can be felt to give lift to the relaxed body
filling the chest
lifting and stimulating sensation in the head
passing out even through the top of the
    cranium
into heaven above
let the inhaled breath
not your muscles
move your body
every inhalation
filling full
every exhalation
emptying out
breathing heaven and earth
canceling out the artificial division
between body and mind
make your exhalations
twice as long as your inhalations
linger for some time

at the top of your inhalation
letting go through the entire body
before you exhale

building on the grounded stability
created through inhaling deeply down
into the lower part of your body
and into the earth below
feel the front of your ribcage billow outward
and soften the tension
in the muscles surrounding the eyes
relax the holding
in the muscles on either side of the cranium
the holding and tension
in each of your eyes
and on either side of your skull
that keep the awakened sensations of radiance
from flowing up through your body
into and out through your head
keep softening the tensions in the cranium
as you hold your breath in
and let it fully out
like a skilled seamstress
thread your needle
through the clamoring voices
on either side of your cranium
each of which is vying for your attention
in a broadcast of egoic banter
your personal Scylla and Charybdis
reaching out to grab you
relaxing tension is the key
to not being grabbed by the mind

and passing through the eye of your needle
transform the cranium
from a still receptacle of thought
into a felt flow of sensations
morphing
bubbling
streaming

uncorking a bottle of sparkling wine
liquid nectar rises up
and fizzes out the top of the bottle
uncorking the wine inside your cranium
the flooding current of sensations
is freed to rush
not only into the cranium from below
but to mushroom up and out through your head
as pleasurable enjoyment
who are you
when you release the tension in the cranium
that keeps the sparkling wine from ever being
  opened
confined to its bottle
its contents never tasted or enjoyed

don't just fall into the earth
or rise up into heaven
stay grounded in the earth
and opened up to heaven's river
at the same time
"I" disappears
into merged sensation vision sound
The Great Wide Open

your natural state
almost unbearably delicious

Conventionally what we call body and what we refer to as mind are viewed as distinctly different entities, the one so solid, dense, and fleshy, the other so invisible and intangible. But this artificial splitting of human experience into two distinct and separate components is a by-product of somatophobia. The mind/body split is actually the natural expression of the quality of consciousness that suppresses radiance. As the shimmer awakens, consciousness has no choice but to morph as well. Your body can't just become radiant on its own with no alteration to your familiar sense of self. When body starts sparking its innate radiance, conventional divisions between body and mind start breaking down. The consciousness of a radiant body ventures beyond its egoic fixation, boundaries, and thought-supported identity.

As a plug gets pulled on silent thought, so does the smoky picture show of self-image—visible only to you, projected out onto a phantom screen, floating just at the front of your face, a window or veil through which you look out onto the world so separate from you—also begin to come apart, literally before your eyes. The practice is not about creating a "Super Me." You have to leave egoic self, and all the imposed tensions that create and support it, momentarily behind. Where previously there was a fixed mental reference point—me—now there's a felt current bubbling, streaming, pulsing, and passing right through the head.

Let It Lead You

just keep relaxing and releasing
the next thought form
that emerges in your cranium
by letting go

the tensions that accompany it
thought reemerges
and wants to take up residence
once again in your cranium
turn the tables
don't let it sneak in
you sneak into it
let it lead you instead
to the precise locus of tension
that can be felt to occupy
the same physical location
to where the thought
can be traced
and then let go
and relax the tension
with the help of the breath
moment to moment
over and over again
let go the tension
on which thought depends

Unlike the butterfly, for whom its caterpillarness is long gone and never again retrievable, you don't have to leave the egoic mind forever behind and can readily use it as you make your way through the world of form. But you also have access to this whole other, completely natural dimension that, in addition to the radically new perspectives on existence that it reveals, is immeasurably more comfortable. Radiance is inherent. It's always been here. It's inside you, just waiting for you to liberate it. It's never something you pump up. It's not a condition that you have to create brick by brick and then piece together. It just needs permission and encouragement to come out to play and then to make its way through the thickets that conventional mind has grown around it.

Ego, the sense that I am an entity named (insert your name here) that has taken up residence in my physical body just like a bird in a cage, gets understandably bad press in the spiritual world as the consciousness of lost in thought is rightly identified as a barrier to awakening. And so the Sufis tell you that "you need to die before you die" and refer to the condition of fana as an "annihilation" of the ego.

Pretty blunt words, and one understands the frustration we all have with a mind that won't shut up, but from a Somatics point of view such a no-holds-barred, direct assault on the ego is unhelpful and even misleading. You don't want to quash your sense of self and cut it out like a malignant tumor. You want to deepen and transform it by softening the inbred tension and holding throughout the body, and especially in the cranium, on which the consciousness of lost in thought depends for its existence. Even more, just as physical pain draws your attention to the exact location where you need to turn your felt attention, so too does the consciousness of lost in thought point you to exactly where you need to go inside your cranium to soften egoic identity and transform it in to The Great Wide Open. When the Sufis tell you that you need to die before you die, what they're really getting at is that the tension, holding, and fixation in the body so responsible for creating your mask needs to relax and unravel so you can come alive while you are alive.

Don't let all this talk of somatic awakening and trans-egoic shimmer leave you thinking that you need to slam the door on any sense of I that rears its head. On the contrary, I is constantly beckoning you, and you would do well to find out where it wants to take you. Go to it. Go right into it, right in the middle of your head, relaxing layer upon emergent layer of *I*, and keep letting go. If you're able to continue letting go of layers and flashes of tension in your cranium, your sense of *I* will keep morphing and shifting, revealing ever deeper layers of *I*.

The cranial journey from egoic fixation to wordless felt presence is reflected in what happens to a pilot who flies a plane through the pounding outer bands of a major hurricane until they arrive at the calm, still center of the storm. Keep penetrating right into the middle of your cranium through all its successive buffeting layers of a sense of *I*, relaxing through each one, until you arrive at a place in the middle of your head that feels the most like you've ever known yourself to be but where the *I* that you familiarly know just seems unfamiliarly absent. *I* becomes a felt flow of constantly morphing and deepening presence rather than a fixed address.

Mystery Space

your first layer
of who you are
your sense of I
is your mask
your persona
that sits right at the front of your face
awash in thought and self-image
locate your mask
feel where it resides
out at the front of the cranium
it's okay to be you
exactly as you are
now go deeper
into your sense of I

back behind your eyes
into the mystery space of your cranium
I am
I am
hopes and fears
that your mask doesn't want to reveal
live here
but the revelations
feel far more authentic
vulnerable
don't stop there
keep going deeper
follow your I
let your sense of I am
lead you
ever deeper inside your cranium
right into the very middle of your head
just let go
and ride the felt waves of unraveling
of the holding patterns of tension
that create the mask
wave after emerging wave
a self image
a thought
comes
on a surge of sensation
it disappears just as quickly
as tension in the cranium lets go
moment after moment
I gets transformed
no longer a fixed point of reference
now morphing

changing
nothing stable
nothing fixed
nothing permanent
let your sense of I
become your vehicle
taking you ever deeper
through successive layers of your mind and
    cranium
until you arrive
at a felt flowing sense
of radiant presence
the bird is freed from its cage

The View

ONE OF THE FIRST THINGS that a teacher from the Dzogchen tradition of Tibet will present to a new student is The View, a conceptual presentation of what the teachings are designed to reveal. In this way the goal of the practice is revealed not at the culmination of years of meditation, but right at the onset, and then the student's work is to enter in to intentional practices that will transform their consciousness, sense of self, and understanding of the nature of reality and reward them with a direct experience of The View. The View is actually an overview, even though conceptual, of where the teachings are ultimately going to lead.

The View of what this little book is calling the *teachings of the radiant body* might be summarized as:

> The quality of consciousness that is viewed as normal keeps you confined to the conceptual realm of the mind. It is, furthermore, essentially disembodied, depending for its existence on the suppression of felt presence. A consciousness so embedded in thought and out of touch with felt presence creates a distorted and limiting belief system about who you are and how reality is constructed. Lodged within the confines of your thinking mind, you naturally view yourself solely as an egoic entity irrevocably separate from everything you perceive to exist outside your physical body.

From the perspective of form alone, this is accurate, but the perspective of form presents only half the reality that could be experienced to exist. Underlying the entire world of form in which every object is distinctly separate from every other object is a vast and cohesive substratum often likened to a vast and empty space that ties everything back together into a single unified piece. You can't conventionally see it the way you see physical objects, but you can directly feel and sense it as you too are an expression of it.

Through the awakening of sensation, the relaxation of tension, and the liberation of breath, the rigid and tense patterns of frozen holding in the soft tissues of the body can start to soften. In place of a consciousness largely lost in thought, identified with the apparent speaker of those thoughts and out of touch with somatic presence, a condition of far more embodied consciousness reveals itself in which sensations shimmer, breath is freed, and the egoic perspective of the mind loosens its authoritarian grip on your experience of self.

And then the whole of the visual field, the entire range of sounds that you can hear in this moment, and the awakened sensations in the entire body collapse down and in to one another and are experienced to merge in to a single, multi-sensorial, coterminous phenomenon. At the moment of that deeply relaxed merging, the radiant shimmer of felt sensation flows through you, the visual field passes in to you, the shifting rivers of sound stabilize you. A fissure in the world of opaque form opens, even if just for a second, and you glide right through in to The Great Wide Open, your fundamental essence and birthright. No longer just an island in a vast sea. Now you become both island and the sea that penetrates everything.

ॐॐ

In addition to this alteration to your sense of self, physical embodiment, and relationship to the wider world, the practices of the radiant body present a whole other, far more literal perspective on what constitutes The View, and this refers to how you look and see.

What do you see? Do you look out onto a world of separation, every object way out there separate from you and from one another as well? Or, through your looking, can you also experience the invisible, underlying substratum that binds every one of those objects together and out of which they appear to emerge? The quality of seeing that helps liberate radiance throughout the body doesn't happen just in the eyes. It happens when you learn to see with your whole body. Or, as Rumi says:

> *don't just look through the eyes of your head*
> *see with the eyes of your soul*

Rumi viewed the body as the physical expression of the inner being, the soul. The soul for Rumi doesn't just shine through the body. It's expressed through the body, and in whatever condition body finds itself, it is that condition at that moment that defines your soul's light. So when Rumi says to see with the eyes of the soul, he points to a way of seeing that is predicated on the awakened, felt shimmer of the body.

What happens to you when you look out upon the world in a body that has softened the tensions in the eyes and is lit up in awakened felt presence?

Look and See

close your eyes
for as long as you like
awaken the shimmer

everywhere throughout the body
a field of vibratory waves of sensation
the whole body felt all at once
now open your eyes
but stay in your awakened shimmer
let the visual field come to you
exactly as it is
don't you reach out to it
gaze at something
anything
an object
a point on the wall
and then . . .
without bringing an iota of tension
back into your cranium . . .
take your vision wide
as wide as you possibly can
so that you become aware of everything
out to the far right and left peripheries
of your visual field
where recognizable objects fade
soften your gaze so you can see
up and down
to the vertical peripheries of your visual
    field
gaze upon the whole of the visual field
a unified field
that you see all at once
an awakened body
that feels the shimmer
from head to foot
can see a unified visual field

feeling everything all at once
seeing everything all at once

as body keeps awakening felt radiance
as you keep softening your gaze
something altogether radical
yet completely natural
begins to occur
visual field and body
formerly so separate
start penetrating one another
merging into one another
joining together
like lovers
unable to keep themselves apart
suddenly visual field is no longer out there
and you exclusively in here
sensation radiates expansively out into visual
     field
visual field enters into you
taking up residence
where thought formerly resided
as Rumi says:
dissolve the body into vision
*become seeing seeing seeing!**

welcome sounds
all sounds near and far
just let sound be heard

---

*This Rumi quote about dissolving the body into vision is cited in *On Having No Head* by Douglas Harding.

sound stabilizes the merging
of sensation and vision
when all three fields
sound
sensation
vision
are experienced simultaneously
in their wholeness
they merge into one another
a breach in the world of appearances
suddenly opens
like a particle of salt
dissolving into water
you dissolve your sense of solely individual
existence
into the greater substratum of union
you leave
even if for only a little moment
the solid shoreline of your I behind
and enter into the river where the I disappears

so long as body keeps allowing
the current of awakened shimmer
to keep passing through it
the whole of the visual field
can merge with it
bind itself to it
enter into it
appear crystal clear
as soon as you enter back into thought
as soon as tension once again disturbs
the free flow of awakened shimmer

the visual field will again separate from you
you will be in here
the visual field will be out there
in this way you move back and forth
in and out
between the consciousnesses
of separation and union

The consciousness of unbidden and random thought and the frozen tension in the cranium that accompanies it directly affect the eyes and how we see. Frozen tensions in the cranium support an ocular setting that can only *see* a world of separation in which everything is divided in to *in here* and *out there*. Melting the tensions throughout the cranium dissolves thought that in turn dissolves the exclusivity of the egoic perspective that then allows you to *see* the world as being of one piece.

A famous Zen koan instructs you to *find your original face before you were born.* In other words, what might your face have been like before *you* took possession of it, before you created the mask, the persona, that you've molded and superimposed onto the soft tissues of your face to create the person you believe yourself to be and want everyone else to believe you are as well?

We create our preferred mask through introducing a sophisticated pattern of tension throughout the cranium. The more tension we import, the further we stray from the altogether natural and original face we were born with. What's behind the mask? What is this mysterious, subtly shimmering, spacious dimension, so integral to who and what you are, so different from who your mask wants you to believe yourself to be? Your original face reveals itself through your natural, relaxed presence. The quality of consciousness that passes as normal is literally an altered state as you insert alterations of tension in to the soft, pliant tissues of your face and cranium.

The Buddha's instructions on breathing—that begin with mindfulness (*as you breathe in, as you breathe out, remain aware of the breath at the front of the body*) and culminate in bodyfullness (*as you breathe in, breathe in through the whole body; as you breathe out, breathe out through the whole body*)—are explored through two differing ways of looking and seeing. Focusing a laser-like attention onto your nostrils as breath passes in and out affects consciousness through a chronic setting of the orbicularis oculi muscles that allow for the narrowing of the eyes. It creates a mind that is one-pointed in itself, concentrated, self-aware. It's the perfect gaze for practicing mainstream mindfulness.

The practices of the radiant body emphasize seeing widely and inclusively. Relaxing the body in to seeing the whole of the visual field all at once has as much effect on consciousness as do the concentration practices. The effect is just very different. The first practice helps you master your incarnation in the world of form. The second explodes you in to The Great Wide Open.

When you're lost in thought and at the effect of the unfelt tensions in your cranium, you sometimes don't even see what's right in front of your eyes. Also as you go off in thought and lose the ability to see the whole of the visual field as a unified field, one eye generally becomes more dominant, creating further energetic imbalance in the cranium.

But when you see the whole of the visual field all at once, this bifurcation between your two eyes essentially heals and resolves itself, and you see not with two separate orbs of vision, but with a unified single gaze. The ability to see the whole of the visual field all at once as a unified sensory field ignites radiance in the body, a phenomenon directly referenced by the historical Jesus:

let your eye be single
and your whole body will be filled with light
MATTHEW 6.22

Light refers to two different, but related, phenomena: weight and vision. Enlightenment (entering into the light) occurs through both the dropping of weight and the awakening of a bodily radiance that others can see. Seeing the whole of the visual field all at once draws you back inside your cranium, behind your eyes, down toward the mysterious feeling presence in the back of your head and neck. The place from which you see globally and impartially—clear, like a mirror, with no mental veil of interpretation, projection, or judgment superimposed onto the visual field—is very closely aligned to where your essential nature is to be found and functions as another invisible doorway in to The Great Wide Open.

We close our eyes to fall asleep at night but then open them again when we awaken in the morning. Nothing could be more natural. I generally begin meditation practice with eyes closed but eventually open them. Buddha means to awaken so at some point in your practice it makes sense for us to open our eyes and engage the visual field.

The best description I have ever heard of the quality of embodied consciousness that the radiant body is privy to is *an undivided wholeness of flowing movement.* What a delicious phrase! When you truly awaken the body and start surrendering to a breath that can indeed *breathe through the whole body*, you gain access to an alternative dimension of consciousness in which your conventional view of separation gives way to reveal a felt ground state of undivided wholeness, a dimension or substratum into which all the separate objects of the universe, including yourself, are irrevocably bonded together. And the way to this awakening of body—and the doorway in to this entrancing dimension of undivided wholeness—is through relaxing so deeply that the body stays in constant, subtle, flowing, amoeba-like movement in resilient response to the breath and the current of the life force.

An undivided wholeness of flowing movement. I wish I'd come up with that phrase myself, but it comes from a far superior source. It's the shorthand phrase that the quantum physicist David Bohm devised to describe how he believes the universe is constructed. Bohm was one of the most respected quantum physicists of the last century, and as his inquiry in to the nature of things deepened, he began to intuit that our understanding of how reality is constructed needed to be radically reconsidered.

For Bohm, there are two fundamental dimensions of reality, what he called the implicate and explicate orders. The implicate order (which he felt had been pretty much completely overlooked by science) was like a unified ground state or source out of which the entire explicate order—with its gajillions of stars and universes and atoms and subatomic particles, all of them constantly moving, twinkling, and shimmering—gets projected, somewhat like how a complex holographic image is projected from a single light source. For Bohm, everything is constantly moving back and forth between these dimensions, but at such a rapid rate that the world of appearances still manages to look solid and stable.

The Heart Sutra, one of Buddhism's most revered texts, in an almost exact prefiguring of Bohm's dual vision of an explicate and implicate order, tells us that everything that exists partakes of two mirrored dimensions: form and emptiness. Permeating the world of form in its infinite multiplicity of separate objects is a substratum of what is often referred to, for lack of better words or terms, as emptiness or space, not the conventional space in which the objects of the world of form are situated, but a kind of nonformal, infinitely extensible, nonsolid dimension of felt reality that all the many different objects in the world of form emerge out from. Everything, including you and me, partakes of both dimensions.

If this sounds too far-fetched or unrelatable, take a moment to regard yourself. Gazing at your reflection in a mirror, you can easily access both these dimensions. On the one hand there's your physical form, the recognizable shape of your face and features. Gazing at yourself from the outside in, your form most definitely looks very solid. But feeling yourself from the inside out presents a whole other dimension of experience. *You* don't feel solid like the book you have in your hand, the chair you sit on, or for that matter the arms of your body that you see holding the book. In fact, inside your body, nothing feels very solid at all. It's more like a kind of shimmering space that permeates and hovers around and inside the solid flesh and bones of your body. It's right there, in a place just behind the screen of your thoughts.

The easiest way to grasp this mind-boggling understanding is to remember that, even though you look at people and recognize them by their very solid looking face and body, you don't experience yourself as particularly solid at all. And if this dual condition of an apparent solidity permeated by an underlying intangible openness is true of you and me, why shouldn't it be true of every other physical object in the universe as well?

The Great Wide Open is what happens when form and emptiness, the explicate and implicate order, are experienced simultaneously. This merged condition of undivided wholeness is very real, but the only way you can directly access it is to make sure that your entire body remains in constant, flowing motion. If you remain stiff and frozen in your body, this extraordinary revelation of dimensions won't appear.

Form and Emptiness

sit or stand in front of a mirror
look at yourself
look at your face
look at its features
its shape
its textures
its eye and skin colors
this is your visible image
that everyone sees
and knows you as . . .
(Nazruddhin went into a bank
the teller asked him for identification
he took a mirror out from his pocket
and looked at his reflection
"yup, it's me alright")
. . . touch your face with your fingers
go ahead and tap your cranium lightly
with a knuckle
rap rap
yup, it's solid alright

now feel into the space inside your cranium
where you feel yourself to be
where you feel that you reside
where you feel who you are
who are you really
and what are you really
from the outside looking in
your body appears solid
from the inside feeling out
not so much

in fact not at all
you feel more
like some kind of
open
spacious
presence
that permeates and pervades
the very solid form
of your physical body

look out onto the visual field
solid objects
occupying their own space
a space that no other object can ever occupy
objects eternally separate
you now know yourself
as solid form
and shimmering emptiness both
look out at the physical objects in front of you
if you're both form and space
so are they
look out onto the visual field
go wide with your vision
and now start feeling in
to the underlying spatial dimension
of the objects in your visual field
both solid object
and underlying substratum
of space and emptiness
just like you
let yourself acknowledge both dimensions
of the visual field

its depiction of solid separate objects
and the immaterial space that completely
     permeates it
let your internal sense of space and emptiness
merge with the space and emptiness
of everything in your entire visual field
so flow on, radiant body
and remember:
constant flowing motion
is what connects you
to the source of all things
right inside you
spreading out from there

Rainbow Body

ONE OF MY FAVORITE IMAGES from Tibetan art is the depiction of the rainbow body (see following page). It represents the culmination of a lifetime of practice during which the practitioner, at the very end of life, dissolves their physical body back in to light. As impossible and far-fetched as this may sound, I've read credible accounts of this phenomenon in the Tibetan literature. A week or so before death, the practitioner announces their intention to assume the rainbow body and enters a specially constructed tent. Ten days later the tent is opened to much celebration by the townspeople, and all that remains on the floor in the center of the tent are the articles of clothing that the practitioner was wearing and perhaps a few hairs and fingernail shavings!

I have no aspirations to attain the rainbow body at the time of my passing. Ordinary death seems just fine to me. However, what I do aspire to, as much as possible, is to manifest a body of radiant presence and light in as many moments of waking life as possible. What might this moment to moment, living version of the rainbow body be like?

Let's go back to the beginning for a moment. Remember that on every part of the body down to the smallest cell, distinct tactile sensations can be felt to exist. Even though these sensations are unimaginably small in size and are oscillating at unimaginably rapid rates of vibratory frequency, they

Nineteenth-century Tibetan thangka of the Nyingma lineage,
depicting the rainbow body of Padmasambhava (center). A body that
experiences its mass as a shimmering flow of vibratory sensations
radiates a quality of glowing light. It becomes literally en-lightened.

Ground mineral pigment on cotton. Private collection. Item number 31903,
Himalayan Art Resources. Unknown Painter.

can still be distinctly felt as a flickering, wave-like shimmer that pervades the entire body. The problem, of course, is that most of the time we have virtually no felt awareness of this shimmer. Because of our religious and cultural conditioning (somatophobia has been alive and well for a very long time), we've had to dim it way down so that we ordinarily feel only a fraction of the sensations that are potentially here to be felt.

But even though we may not feel them, sensations are here for the feeling all the time, and all you need to do for sensations to start reappearing is to turn your attention to them and welcome them back to felt life. As soon as you remember and give yourself permission to shift in to feeling awareness, sensations start coming out of hiding, emerging awakened from their long, dry sleep of unfelt hibernation. If you keep on doing this, moment after moment, hour after hour, a time can come when the entire body becomes sensationalized: streaming flows of bright, shimmering, tactile wavelets of sensation spreading through and radiating out from the body. A highly creative and artistic image of such a condition would look to me a whole lot like the depiction of the rainbow body.

If all this talk of rainbow bodies sounds too sensational, well . . . remember that sensations are literally sensational.

I have no idea if attaining the rainbow body at the moment of death is possible or even desirable. I do know that, were such a thing to occur, it would have had to have been based on a lifetime of remembering, as best one can, to constantly welcome the feeling presence emanating out of each and every cell of the body back to felt life.

Rainbow Embodiment

sit down in meditation posture
start with your eyes closed
play with The Line
evoke relaxation
let go into the natural motions
that the body spontaneously makes
sit in radiance
awakened waves of felt shimmer
flowing everywhere throughout the body
open your eyes
when the whole of the body shimmers
so does the whole of the visual field
appearing before you
begin to sparkle and shimmer as well
feel body and vision
begin to penetrate one another
in intertwining shimmer
sensations expanding outward
in all directions
like streams of radiant light
touching into the visual field
vision penetrating inward
filling up the space
that thought has so recently vacated
let radiant streams of sensation
expand in all directions
touching into every little pixel
of the visual field
both seen in front
and unseen behind

All of the practices presented in this book are here to help you remember, to wake up from the amnesia that's left you unaware of your intrinsic felt radiance. They certainly have that effect on me whenever I remember to remember. Right now, this very moment, is the only time frame in which you can ever choose to remember. As we will see in the next chapter, it's all about right now.

This Very Body

all beings from the very beginning of time are buddhas
it's like water and ice
apart from water there can be no ice
apart from living beings there can be no buddhas
realizing the great wide open as your essential nature
the gate opens
you go to a place beyond words
feeling into the emptiness
that permeates all form
you'll always be at home
wherever you are
dropping down into the silence beneath thought
truth can only be spoken in the language of dance and song
wide is your heaven
radiant your moon
what more could you ask for
the ultimate state appears
this very place the lotus paradise
this very body the buddha

HAKUIN EKAKU (1686–1769)
(I have added small tweakings to the traditional
translation of Hakuin's "Song of Meditation")

One of my earliest childhood memories is of a comic book in which a heroic figure suddenly awakens from a long and fitful sleep to find himself transported in to a vast desert valley, and he understands with certainty that his task now is to find his way home. He has no idea how he got here. All he knows is that this is no dream. He's stuck in this alien world, and he needs to get back home.

He looks all around him. The alien world of the desert is vast, and a hundred miles away in every direction, circling the entire valley, is a mountain range with apparently vertical cliffs that he knows he will need to climb to free himself from his predicament. And so he sets out.

After many days have passed, he arrives at the foot of the sheer, vertiginous cliffs and begins scaling them, one carefully placed foot at a time, with no safety ropes. It is dauntingly difficult, but after a long and arduous climb, he reaches the top and pulls himself up. And looks around.

He's not back home. He's in an even larger valley with steeper mountains in the distance completely encircling this new desert wasteland. He's human, so of course there's a moment of disappointment. But he's heroically human as well, and so he lets his disappointment go and sets out once again, walking across the burning sands in the direction of a mountain he hopes he can climb. With every step he takes he knows with certainty that he is one step closer to home.

I don't know why I remember this particular comic, but its image of waking up in a predicament, resolving to extricate yourself from it, only to encounter a next deeper layer of challenge has always seemed to me to be a well-crafted metaphor for the practices of the radiant body. First we awaken to the fact that we've been born in to the mystery of a physical body. Then we acknowledge the predicament this body finds itself in which—in this culture at this time—is how lost we are in our thoughts and how out of touch we are with the feeling presence of our body. And then we set out to resolve the imbalances implicit in this condition.

With the help of The Line, we set out to awaken the body, to invite the sensations—the tingling, vibratory, shimmering buzz—in every cell of the body to come out of hiding and unfelt hibernation and come back to vibrant felt life. We immediately greet their acceptance of our invitation, as soon as they enter the front door of felt awareness, with a gesture of relaxation. We keep relaxing through the body's mass, and the body spontaneously keeps moving even on our meditation cushion.

Perhaps we've spent preliminary time focusing on our breath as a way to begin calming the out of control parade of thoughts that's replaced the feeling presence of the body and sent that presence in to exile. Then we start letting go and welcoming felt sensation back in to awareness. As recorded in the early texts of Theravadin Buddhism, we awaken the feeling presence referred to as *vedana*. But we don't just open to sensation in a body that is frozen and stiff. We work to relax the tensions in the body as much as possible through playing with upright balance as we sit and meditate. Gradually the armoring and barriers that keep the vibratory presence of soma contained and locked behind walls of tension both painful and numb begin to soften and melt.

Building on this extraordinary preliminary foundation, we can now begin to let go, breath by breath, sensation by sensation, and we realize that soma is more like a current in a river than a stable, flickering buzz. And here's where our meditation practice evolves onto a whole new level as we're called upon to surrender to soma's current, to allow a completely natural, organic, and nondirected surrender to start occurring in which the holding and tension in the body and mind start—in their own way and in their own time and through their own movements—to unravel. Layer upon layer of holding and tension come to the surface—just as an ever new valley awaited the heroic figure from my comic—and we let go to the current of the new appearance and allow it to begin to move us. Resisting soma's current is the primary cause of chronic pain and confused mind. It's why we find ourselves in the alien valley in the first place.

This.

It always starts with *this*. It proceeds through *this*. It culminates in *this*.

This inhalation. This sensation. This exhalation. This motion. This moment.

This very body the Buddha.

Buddha can only be found in *your* body, in your body. Nowhere else. In fact, Buddha has always been present in your body. But for your very body to be Buddha, as the Zen teacher and poet Hakuin declares to be so, you need to be in your body, you need to experience it directly, you need to learn its language and listen to what it's telling you (it speaks through felt sensation, not thought), you need to allow the spontaneous motions that want to occur, and far too much of the time we're out of touch with the feeling presence that is our body. Out of touch with body, we lose contact with this *this* that we are.

From the perspective of a consciousness lost in thought and out of touch with the shimmer, the declaration that your body and the consciousness of Buddha are one and the same seems, frankly, pretty far-fetched, absurd even. But if you can awaken your body from its slumber of numbness, if you can resurrect the vibratory shimmer, the felt energetic glow and flow of sensations, then your body becomes a vehicle through which the awakened consciousness that the Buddha told us is both our birthright and destiny can naturally express itself in and through you. Your very body the Buddha. But you have to get in touch with *this* first. You have to awaken feeling presence, and the feeling presence of body can only be felt and known in *this* moment.

> *radiance can only be felt*
> *in this moment*
> *radiance remembered*
> *is not radiance*
> *radiance in the future*
> *is not radiance*

Hakuin's poem begins with melting the frozen tensions in the body back in to softer tissue, like melting ice in to water, and ends with the remarkable statements that this very place in which you find yourself, the very body you were born to, are potentially both paradise and your awakened state.

Can you simply relax in to seeing everything that you can see right now, hearing everything that's here to be heard right now, feeling the awakened shimmer of sensations that pervades the entire body in this moment? If you can, you create a mandala of paradise to look out onto. Not the high mountains, not the rivers and lakes, not the primeval forests, not the perfect accessories, not the perfect anythings. Just *this*, where you are right now, exactly as it appears, opened to and embraced. See everything at once, just as it is, and you're in paradise. Invite feeling presence to come back alive, and you awaken Buddha in you.

Out of touch with our body, suppressing its natural felt radiance, body becomes a pale thing, a solidified object, a concept at arms length, but conceptions about the body are radically different from the direct felt experience of the body. We live in a culture that fears the land mines of interior energetic forces just waiting to explode open and expose our inability to keep these forces contained. And we dislike how feeling presence keeps constantly knocking at our doors of awareness, seeking entry, while we attempt to mold ourselves into self-images that are a pallid reflection of our natural vibratory presence. We want to present ourselves to the world in a certain way, as a certain kind of character and individual, that everyone can immediately recognize, and we want very much to believe that this is indeed who we are. A Type-A Wall Street lawyer? A Hollywood seductress? Perhaps as a good father, a violent gang member with street credentials, an exemplar of your religious beliefs? The roles are endless.

But the way we want to be seen by the world is not the *this* that Hakuin is pointing to. The problem with enacted personas is that they have to manipulate and alter the natural state of the body, the free flow of sensations, the *this*, and turn it in to a *that*. And whenever body gets manipulated so its expression is more in accordance with a chosen persona, you forfeit the this that Hakuin tells us is your very body, the this that is synonymous with your radiant, awakened state.

This can always and only be located by contacting where you are right now. And so the first clue on how to embark on this meditational journey of somatic awakening and surrender is that you have to turn your felt awareness to your body, tune in to where you actually are right now, and start there. You can't force the body to be different than it is. You can't force sensations to be different from how they are. You just feel in to the reality of body as it is, right now, engage the practices, and then ride upon the sensations that start awakening and the currents that morph and change what you experience right now into ever new versions of right now, ever new manifestations of *this*, and on and on.

It's my sincere hope that the words and suggestions in this book have revealed to you an alternative path to the traditional exploration of Buddhist teachings, one that focuses more on the simple sensations of the body than the elaborate workings of the mind. The term *buddha*, after all, means to awaken, and what is so very asleep and in need of awakening and resurrecting is the felt shimmer of the body. For the dharma to implant itself successfully into Western culture, it needs to go back to its roots of awakening. Sensations are here to be felt all the time but we don't feel them. Why don't we feel them? What happens when you waken from the sleep of the body? Awakening is not something that can ever happen just in the mind. Awakening is felt throughout the entire body as sensation comes back to felt life. All too often we hear stories of unending physical pain coming out of Vipassana retreat, Zen sesshin, Vajrayana dhatun. With little to no instruction on how to sit in comfort and grace, the practices for far too many people generate a prolonged and crushing ache that we accept, I guess, as the price of admission to get closer to the wisdom teachings (even as it keeps you estranged from them). But this piece of pain is NOT NECESSARY, and it doesn't take you deeper into the teachings. It makes it harder for you to experience what the teachings are telling you. For the dharma truly to take root and establish itself in the new world of the West the practices need to become far more user-friendly, and the path of the radiant body shows you precisely how to do that. Taking these suggestions to heart, the conquering hero may turn out not to be the one who manages to subdue the dragons of the mind, but the bound slave wriggling to break free, figuring out how to surrender to the awakened current of ever unfolding sensations that is the body.

AFTERWORD

The Birthing of Western Dharma

EVERY TIME BUDDHISM HAS MIGRATED to a new territory it has always incorporated into its body of teachings the psychological issues and needs of the culture into which it's moving, and in this way a new facet to the dharma jewel is created. The dharma interacts with the austere samurai culture of Japan, and Zen is birthed. The teachings arrive on the Tibetan plateau where they encounter the florid shamanism of the Indigenous Bon-po people, and the uniquely Tibetan version of the Vajrayana is created out of the mix. Buddhism is coming to the West, and there is no way that a uniquely Western form of Buddhism won't be created. How can we continue to honor the essence of the teachings while addressing the unique issues, needs, and realities of the Western world? And how can we reform what we view as the areas of rigidity in which traditional dharma has gone astray? In many ways this book has been a response to these questions, and the following principles directly address this new birthing:

1. Ours is a culture lost in thought and out of touch with the felt presence of the body. The primary focus of Western Dharma will be the resurrection of the felt, vibratory presence of body, for as body reawakens and comes back

119

to felt life, unbidden and random thought diminishes into silence and you slip on in to a radically different, but altogether natural, dimension of being. Who do you become when body awakens and conventional mind melts? Western Dharma will support you on your journey of discovery to the answer to that question.

2. Much of the Buddhism coming over from Asia has painted itself into a corner of frozen stillness that only serves to subvert the transformation that we hope meditation will enact. The purpose of meditation—as beautifully expressed in the opening quotation to this book—is to wake up and come alive, not to become like a stone garden statue of the Buddha. Frozen stillness is the antithesis of wakefulness and aliveness. Western Dharma, focusing as it will on the awakening of the felt presence of body, will become a literally ecstatic practice, ecstasy being understood as an ex-stasis, a coming out of the condition of frozen stillness in which altogether natural, constant, spontaneous, subtle motion in resilient response to the awakened unfolding of breath and current can occur throughout the entire body.

3. Breath will no longer remain an object of observation but will evolve in to a subject of transformation. In this way Western Dharma will present a path that takes on the challenge of the Buddha's culminating instruction on breath: *to breathe through the whole body.* Most contemporary Buddhism focuses on the Buddha's opening instruction to remain aware of the breath but never proceeds to the culminating instruction. The understanding of what constitutes liberation will come back down to earth and refer to what occurs when you begin to liberate the breath from its imprisonment in unnecessarily held and inert flesh.

4. The Bhagwan (Holy One) paradigm for teaching will be replaced by the Maitreya (Friend) paradigm, just as the historical Buddha prophesied would happen at exactly this time. Teachers, both Eastern and Western, who inadvertently encourage adoration from their students continue to get themselves in trouble. In particular, the transition from the conservative, and sexually suppressed, monastic cultures of Asia in to the libertine culture of the West has proved disastrous for far too many teachers. At the same time students need to take more responsibility for their own transformation and quit acting like giddy groupies around rock and roll gods.

5. We live at a time when the availability of entheogenic substances (cannabis, LSD, psilocybin, MDMA, ayahuasca, mescaline, ibogaine) is becoming widespread throughout our culture. Emerging research suggests that plant substances may have played a significant role in the creation of Hinduism and the Vajrayana, and Western Dharma will recommit to Buddhism's goal of exploring the far reaches of consciousness and recognize that its attitude of just saying no to entheogenic substances is both regressive' and reactionary.

The cutting edge of the psychotherapy world is currently exploring the extraordinary potential of the above-named substances for healing PTSD, addictions, and trauma that have remained intractable to more traditional modalities of intervention. The same open and exploratory attitude to substances is also true for the cutting edge of the dharma. If these substances can generate near miraculous healings in psychotherapy patients, why shouldn't they have a similar effect on the practice of meditation?

One of the differences between the psychotherapeutic and dharma worlds in their approach to entheogens has to do with dosage. Psychotherapy commonly employs large doses that can be best tolerated and explored by patients if they lie down on their backs in a controlled environment. Smaller mini-doses of the same substances allow meditators to remain upright for long periods of time and support the approach to sitting practices presented in this book.

This does not mean that these substances will become a required staple of practice but that protocols will be established for their safe and responsible use for those people who wish to explore them in the context of meditation practice. In light of this, Western Dharma will most likely create two parallel somatic legs. The first will continue to promote the approach of the traditions and eschew any mind-altering substances because that's what works best for many people. The second will explore how to use these substances safely and effectively as catalysis for meditation practices, also because that's what works best for many people.

If you're someone for whom entheogens work well as allies on your path of awakening, and if you live in a community in which these substances are legal or are willing to risk violating current law to follow your heart's impulse, you can take the doses currently favored by the psychotherapeutic community either in a formal therapeutic environment or outdoors, either alone or with a close friend (remember: The Friend is now the form of your teacher) in nature. Over and above the extraordinary revelations that can occur through large doses, they teach you very directly how to let go. And then you will want to only consume mini-doses of the same substances when you sit and explore radiant body meditation practices.

The practices presented in this book work equally well for both the more traditional and more entheogenic paths of sitting meditation.

6. While sitting remains the preferred posture for meditative practice, Western Dharma will balance out long hours of sitting with dynamic physical practices such as hatha yoga, martial arts, aerobics, Pilates, resistance training, 10,000 steps, ecstatic dance, Five Tibetan Rites, gardening, walking your dog, anything really that moves the body and increases your heart rate. Is there a best, preferred form of exercise to complement your sitting practice? Yes. It's the one you feel the most drawn to.

7. Because the primary orientation of Western Dharma will be the awakening of felt presence throughout the entire body, and because this awakening is so foreign to so many of us, students will be encouraged to explore the offerings of Somatic therapists as catalyst for their meditational practices. To mention but a few: Rolfing Structural Integration can be enormously supportive in helping a meditator find a posture that is upright, relaxed, and resiliently moving; therapies like Hakomi and Somatic Experiencing can help expose and release residues of trauma and abuse from the body; the powerful breathing practices of Rebirthing and Holotropic Breathwork can help melt blockages to the natural fullness of breath; entheogenic psychotherapy can, often quite rapidly, pinpoint and resolve attitudes of mind, body, and emotion that keep you stuck in the quality of mind that we look to the dharma as providing a way out of.

ADDENDUM

Hollow Bamboo Breathing

FOR THE LAST NUMBER OF YEARS I've been exploring and refining an extremely potent breathing practice. What I'm calling Hollow Bamboo Breathing (from Tilopa's exhortation *to become like a hollow bamboo*) is an adaptation of a little known Burmese form of Vipassana called Sunlun that I've modified and expanded to more compatibly support the practices and goals of radiant body meditation: the establishment of a posture that's upright, relaxed, and resiliently motile; the awakening of felt, shimmering presence throughout the body; the surrender to a breath that can be felt to move through the entire body; the cleansing of emotional blockages, the melting of the egoic fixation of the mind, and the natural entrance in to the birthright state I call The Great Wide Open. Hollow Bamboo Breathing powerfully supports all these goals and has four phases, each of them fifteen minutes long.

PHASE ONE
. . . .
Summoning the Helpers

Sit down on your meditation seat—be it cross-legged on supporting cushions and floor mats, on a kneeling bench, or in a chair. Make sure your pelvis is higher than your knees to create a stable base over which the upright torso can float. Start feeling your way in to The Line. Sit up as tall as you can be but as relaxed as you can be. Pass your feeling awareness through your entire body, over and over again, inviting felt sensation and presence to awaken and relax. Let breath create movement through your entire body, like an amoeba expanding on the inhalation, contracting on the exhalation. Become your awakened sensations and breath.

PHASE TWO
· · · · · · · · ·
Journeying on the Breath

Start breathing forcibly and rapidly through the nose and/or mouth. Take about two strong breaths a second. Sometimes you find that you're breathing more through the mouth or through the nose. Sometimes you find that you're accenting the inhalation, other times the exhalation.

As you surrender in this way to the breath, it's VERY important that you keep the entire body in constant motion. Begin by accenting the motions of *Undulating Breath*. On the sharp inhalation the pelvis and lumbar spine rock forward; on the exhalation they move backward. The head is in constant motion, bobbing up and down to the rhythms of the breath. The entire spine undulates like a fly fishing rod in rapid motion. Surrender to the breath and the movement breath inspires.

Start letting whatever movements want to occur to express themselves freely as you continue to sit on your cushion, chair, or kneeling bench. The body may gyrate from side to side, rotating around The Line. The legs may tense and release as though you're riding a horse. The hands may shake. Surrender into a spontaneous dance, and ride the motions deep inside your body where long unexpressed primal feelings live.

The strong breath gives you an opportunity to let go completely in to The Line. Areas of blockage, both physical and emotional, start revealing themselves. Let everything come: ecstasy, sadness, fear, rage, anything. As deep primal states arise, breath will change its rhythms and body may start taking on the frozen postures of these deep states. This second phase of Hollow Bamboo Breathing is more a journey in to your deep self than it is a breathing exercise.

Feel the breath touching everywhere in your body. Don't be tame. The breath will change according to whatever it's bringing up: old memories, elation, pain, emotion, strong sensation. With every breath you can feel a cleansing happening through the long interior shaft of the body. The stronger the surrendered breath the deeper you go into yourself: bottomless sadness, beaming happiness, feral rage (the Lion's Roar spoken of by the Tibetans is more akin to Janov's primal scream than a kitten's meow). Don't fish for any kind of cathartic release. Just keep letting go and be with whatever comes, however strong or mild it may be.

PHASE THREE
· · · · · · · · · ·
Surrendering to Current

At the end of fifteen minutes, exhale through your mouth as deeply as you can and empty your lungs as completely as you can. The body will curl down into a C-curve, your head will fall forward, and you will rotate back behind your pelvis as you forcibly push out every last little bit of used air in your lungs. Keep pushing the air out, and feel the belly and chest tense to force out the last bit of breath. Hold your breath out as long as you can. Then let go through your entire body and breathe in as deeply as you can. Start by breathing in through your nose and then complete the breath by breathing through your mouth. Your torso will uncoil from its collapsed position in to a strong and long upright posture. After the initial surrender to the incoming breath keep opening to as full an inhalation as you possibly can by taking a final few short, sharp sipping breaths to fill your body completely. Now hold your breath in for as long as you possibly can. Keep relaxing the body as you hold the breath in, and let whatever wants to happen happen.

Now let it out, surrender in to your exhalation, and then just continue to let yourself breathe in whatever way is natural for you.

Your body will be vibrating strongly from the Phase Two breathing, so just sit and let go. Let strong currents and flows of sensation and emotion build and subside throughout this phase. Ride the changing flows and presence of the feeling body. Feel the vibratory nature of your body as a flame burning up everything that restricts your radiance. If you start feeling too adrift in your thoughts, resummon the helpers of The Line: awakened radiance and undulation. Perhaps explore the practice of Virtual Acupuncture: The Portal Meditation and Breathing in the Six Directions, the koan that *a body is something wrapped around the breath; let the wraps flow freely like silk scarves.* When you can once again feel your entire body all at once as a unified field of shimmer, just let go. You may want to open your eyes, embrace vision and sound, and play with The Great Wide Open.

PHASE FOUR
• • • • • • • • •
Dissolving

Lie down on your back, your arms at your side. Feel the whole body and mind surrendering its weight to gravity's tug in conjunction with a long and extended exhalation. However breath wants to breathe, let it breathe you that way, and just keep letting go. The body will continue to tingle and shimmer, but your breath will eventually slow way down, and you may even fall asleep on a long, extended exhalation.

ஔ∾ஔ

A more complete *sadhana* (spiritual practice) might have you exploring the practices of the radiant body for an hour, taking an hour break from sitting and going for a brisk walk or run, doing yoga or chi kung, Kum Nye or Pilates, the Five Tibetan Rites, spontaneous dance, whatever you do as your preferred form of exercise, and then sitting down again for a final hour of Hollow Bamboo Breathing. Perhaps once a month you can take an entire day just for yourself and do this full sadhana two or even three times during the day. It's extremely powerful and works to awaken the unfelt body, heal chronic pain, and melt the primal contraction at the center of body and mind.

Acknowledgments
and Further Study

I WAS FORTUNATE TO STUDY with Ida Rolf in the mid-1970s. While you won't be surprised to hear that she was my most important bodywork teacher, you may be more surprised to hear that I've always considered her one of my very most important spiritual teachers as well. While she knew that the work had enormous potential to help heal the pains of the body, she had larger visions in mind. As a young woman she had studied tantric yoga with a spiritual community in upstate New York, and she directly understood that real healing was not just about making the pain go away and feeling better but evolving in to an alternate condition of consciousness that the pain was obscuring. I never heard her use the word *spiritual*. She would speak of *evolution* instead. It was from her that I was first introduced to the concept of The Line and understood how important it was in the evolution of human consciousness. She would suggest that, if a body can find its way to a more effortless upright stance within the field of gravity, that body could let go of unnecessary tension. Like a stone dropping into a pool of water and causing a large splash, the dropping away of unnecessary tension would liberate what she called *evolutionary energies* that would then spread through the whole body resulting in a transformation of human consciousness. In many ways this is the primary foundational principle I bring to the world of Buddhist meditation.

The young men and women that were drawn to her were her children/guinea pigs/lab rats, and she liked to hear our accounts of what would occur in our personal experiments with exploring The Line. She didn't really want to hear about the drugs that often seemed to catalyze those experiments—mostly cannabis, LSD, psilocybin, and MDA—but she was keen to hear what was happening to us. In those early days there were a couple of ex-Jesuit brothers who were like acolytes to her, openly sharing that through working with her methods they had come much closer to Christ consciousness than during their years in the Jesuit order.

From the other genius from the Rolf world, Judith Aston, I first understood how important it was to keep the body in motion. I owe both these teachers a profound debt of gratitude for exposing me to ideas that I would have never likely considered on my own.

Unless otherwise noted, quotations from Rumi are my own translations that I created in partnership with Nevit Ergin, the Turkish doctor and spiritual philosopher who is the primary source of bringing Rumi to the English speaking world.

Credible accounts of practitioners entering the rainbow body come from the Dzogchen teacher Namkhai Norbu.

No acknowledgement section would be complete without a special *gasho* to Coco, my wife and partner in the practices, who, as Hakuin suggested, speaks in the language of dance and song and delightfully reminds me every day that The Great Wide Open isn't just a sensed phenomenon of sensation and space but possesses a profound, intrinsic emotional tone called love.

While this book represents the culmination of my understanding about how awakening works, many of my former books go into more specific detail about different aspects of the awakening:

The Posture of Meditation, 2nd Edition
Breathing through the Whole Body
Eyes Wide Open
Rumi's Four Essential Practices

Finally, anyone wishing to contact me or receive announcements of retreats and programs directly relating to the awakening of the radiant body may do so at **www.embodiment.net**.

Index

Page numbers in *italics* refer to illustrations.